Acclaim for *The Business Co*

"*The Business Coaching Handbook* is packed full of extremely useful information. I found the ideas the inspiration I needed for taking my business to the next level. There are many different practical business models which are explained clearly and were easy to apply. Time has always been a challenge for me and it was an eye-opener to discover the ways I waste time. The variety of techniques I now employ when organising my time has given me the space to work on growing the business."
– *Jo Down*. Dartmoor Horse Trails
www.dartmoor-holiday-cottages.co.uk

"This book works as a business owners conscience and a wake up call, all in one. It reminds business owners of what they said they would do and have not yet achieved. It also introduces new ideas and methodologies for overcoming those troublesome little challenges which are so easy to avoid taking any action on until they have grown so big they have become a crisis. Every business owner should take time to read this book and if you are short on time – read chapter 3!"
– *Carmine De Leso*, Director Winemaking & Production,
HM Wines International Pty Ltd *www.henrymartinwines.com*

"Without doubt Curly Martin is in the vanguard of a movement for change which is totally in tune with the current business climate. Her depth of knowledge and insight have proved to be an invaluable tool for me in the success and expansion of my Company. I am sure that by reading *The Business Coaching Handbook*, and most importantly taking the action required, both existing and prospective entrepreneurs will achieve the results to which they aspire. Highly recommended!"
– *Margaret Edmondson*, Director, Edmondson & Company Ltd

"Curly's clarity of thinking coupled with her ability to apply personal development concepts to real world situations has proved invaluable in both my personal and business life. I would have no hesitation in recommending her work to any aspiring entrepreneur looking to leverage some quality ideas in their business."
– *Nigel Winship*, Managing Director, 1st Thought,
www.1st-thought.com

The Business Coaching Handbook

Everything You Need to be Your Own Business Coach

Curly Martin

Crown House Publishing Limited
www.crownhouse.co.uk
www.chpus.com

First published by

Crown House Publishing Ltd
Crown Buildings, Bancyfelin, Carmarthen, Wales, SA33 5ND, UK
www.crownhouse.co.uk

and

Crown House Publishing Company LLC
6 Trowbridge Drive, Suite 5, Bethel, CT 06801-2858, USA
www.CHPUS.com

British Library Cataloguing-in-Publication Data
A catalogue entry for this book is available
from the British Library.

10 Digit ISBN 184590060x
13 Digit ISBN 978-1845900601

LCCN 2006939035

All stories in this book are true but the names of the individuals
concerned have been changed

Printed and bound in the UK by
Cromwell Press, Trowbridge, Wiltshire

To my mother, a great business entrepreneur
who still inspires and instructs me,
even though she is in her eighties.

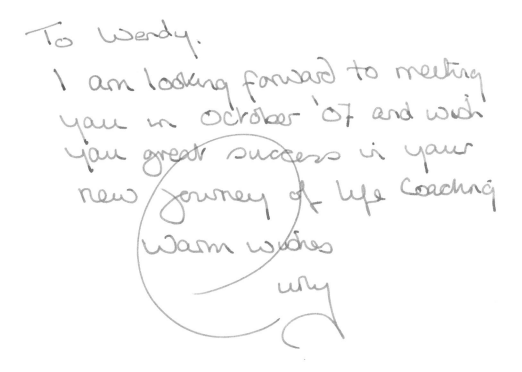

To Wendy.

I am looking forward to meeting
you in October '07 and wish
you great success in your
new journey of life Coaching

Warm wishes

why

Table of Contents

Acknowledgements

Jackie Fletcher for proofreading expertise and curiosity. Colin Edwards for all his literary advice and wizardry, which provided the means for this work to get to the publishers. Mary Edwards for her support of Colin. Ted Edmonson for his enthusiasm.

Ric Hayman for his patience in the boiler room.

Paul Sandy for his great photography.

For my family and friends who understand the challenges I encountered while managing a successful business and writing a book simultaneously.

My husband for his love and support.

Introduction

A very personal letter from the author

This introduction is a vital part of the book.

Even if you typically skip pages like this, now is a great time to change the habits of a lifetime, because many of the following chapters will encourage you to make similar changes to your attitudes and beliefs about business. If you are totally new to the business world, they will ensure that you embark on the correct course from day one.

This introduction will help you get the optimum benefits from the ideas and concepts that follow, so stay with it for a few moments longer.

The Fun Begins

This book has been compiled for business entrepreneurs who have recently achieved the first goal of getting the enterprise up and running, or have been operating their own professional practice or business for a few years and now want to take it to the next level. It can also be very beneficial if you are just dreaming about going it alone by creating your own business.

I recommend that you start with a glance through the synopses of each chapter first, so that you can prioritise or select those that are the most meaningful to you at the moment. If you have recently reviewed your current business and now have clear goals to work on, you can select the most appropriate chapters to support your plans. Perhaps you have been thinking of making some changes and want some inspiration or ideas on how to generate more money – if so, simply select the chapter for your immediate needs. Your focus and needs will change as your business changes and evolves, and you will certainly change your priorities too.

If you have borrowed this book, apart from questioning your commitment, it is important that you return it to its owner in good condition, so resolve now to order your own copy today. If you have bought this copy, thank you and congratulations! Now I am about to send you shopping again.

It can be infuriating to read a good idea and then be unable to find it again later, so I invite you to buy a set of three coloured highlighter pens. As you read, use a traffic light system to mark the sections that apply to you. For example, you could select red for 'must do' items, yellow for 'should do soon' and blue for 'OK at the moment but may need attention soon'. Keep a pen with the book too, and then you can circle your significant page numbers as an additional rapid reference guide.

Ideas will come to you as you read and may well be forgotten by the time you turn the page. Ideas are as fragile as fluffy white clouds on an otherwise clear summer day, and will vanish almost before you can say 'look at that'. Any one of those ideas could be a breakthrough moment of 'Aha' rainbow brilliance and far too valuable to lose, so acquire a notebook and use it to capture key word reminders of your ideas as you read. Then refer to it later when you have time to develop your ideas further.

DIAGNOSTIC QUESTION BOX

What are your plans for taking your business to the next level?

Within each chapter are diagnostic question boxes which are designed to make you think about your business and prompt you to consider what could be done to improve it. Spend time with the questions and write the answers in your notebook along with any actions you need to take.

At the end of each chapter there is a diagnostic action box along with a final page dedicated to your personal action boxes. These are designed to encourage you to commit to taking actions on the ideas and strategies you will have read. The diagnostic action box has suggestions of actions you might need to take. The last page of each chapter requires you to write the actions you want to take and to identify the dates by which you will have achieved them. The personal action boxes are deliberately small because they should work as an aide-mémoire and motivator. Make

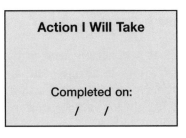

more detailed observations in your notebook as soon as ideas are generated. Using the action boxes and the notebook simultaneously will hold you to your commitments and act as your silent coach.

I have already given you several simple instructions and you will come across many more in each chapter. I have introduced them this early to establish a pattern. I can coach you to coach yourself, but unless you take positive action, we are both wasting our time. There, I have said it, that magic word 'coach'. Coaching may not be magic, but the outcomes it can create may seem nothing less than magical. This is an opportune moment to define what I mean by coaching.

Coaching Simplicity

You will probably have come across coaching in a sporting context – business coaching and life coaching work just as effectively and in similar ways.

Your coach cannot do the work for you but can, and should, suggest where you direct your focus to gain the optimum benefit from doing what you do. Self analysis without a support system can be difficult and demoralising. Coaching looks at what you are doing, examines how you are doing it and asks why you are doing it that way. Coaching is not about the past, it is about where you are now and where you want to be by some defined future date.

It clearly follows that you can only start a journey from where you are now and your journey to business success follows this rule. Similarly, you must have a clear destination in mind otherwise you will drift off course and, even worse, will not know when you have arrived!

That is coaching in a nutshell. Whether you opt for self coaching or invite external help, it is all about knowing where you are, where you are going and the actions that you will take to get there. Coaching is not a quick fix, it is a process.

The most effective coaching provides a drip-feed of constant and continuous information to fuel your motivation, to plan and make any changes that are needed, and to keep you on track by making the most of what you have. This leads to another simple instruction. Please set aside a regular period each day to spend time with your book, notebook and pen. Even five minutes is better than nothing and ten minutes is even better, especially if you add another five minutes to digest and consider what you have read. Spend time each day to plan and write down the actions you will take – no matter how small the steps may seem, they will to lead you towards your goals, aims and objectives.

If you keep doing the same things in the same ways, you will always achieve the same results. If those results are exactly what you want, then congratulations, but ask yourself why you picked up this book in the first place. Are they truly and exactly what you want? If not, then the following chapters offer you a series of signposts to point you in the right direction of change.

Effective coaching uses metaphors, examples and analogies to deliver results. That is why you will find a brief real-life story to launch each chapter. As they say in some movies, "The stories are true, only the identities have been changed to protect the innocent."

Are you ready to start writing and living your own story? It has a two-word title, Business Success. You will notice the second letter of each word. There will be no b*u*siness s*u*ccess without *you* and your positive actions.

Due Diligence

You will probably come across 'due diligence' sooner rather than later in your business career. It is often linked with the slightly odd sounding, 'doing due diligence'.

This is what all buyers should do before agreeing to any transaction, whether they are buying a book, a car or even a company. In plain language, you 'do due diligence' when you flick through the pages in a bookshop, when you take a test drive or when you examine a company's financial records. What you are doing is satisfying yourself that the objects of your desire meet your needs, are fit for the purpose and represent good value.

This is your responsibility. You may seek the advice of people who should know, you may include personal recommendations in your decision, but ultimately the buck stops with you. You take responsibility for your actions, fully and totally.

It is sometimes claimed that we live in a society of blame culture. As far as your business or career success is concerned, forget about blame. Your personal life is down to you alone. Your business life is down to you alone. All the decisions you make are down to you alone. And guess who is going to apply the principles, tips and hints in this book!

Remember this saying: "If it is to be, it is up to me!"

The advice and information in this book is based on over 20 years'

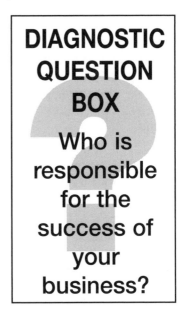

DIAGNOSTIC QUESTION BOX

Who is responsible for the success of your business?

practical experience as a corporate business coach. I am now the owner of a very successful coaching and coach training business, which has been operating successfully for over ten years, but I am not a lawyer, an accountant nor a medical person. You need to know this because what you are about to read complies with English law at the time of publication.

Laws are changed from time to time and many cases that come to court are won or lost according to recent precedent and the skills of barristers. In legal, financial and health matters you *must* always seek the services of appropriately trained and qualified professionals as part of your personal due diligence. Because I have no control over the way that you use the information in these pages, your due diligence must also recognise that you alone are responsible for compliance with local rules and regulations, with governmental obligations and, equally importantly, for the outcomes of any actions that you take. This book is a valuable guide, but remember, the responsibility for the way that you apply it is yours!

A Special Bonus

When you have read this book and applied the ideas and suggestions in each chapter, you may still feel that your personal circumstances could benefit from personal input from a professional coach working with you in a one-on-one session or two. As a special bonus, you can email your contact details (in absolute commercial confidence) to Achievement Specialists and a member of our coaching team will reply with a time and date for an introductory chat, which will be free of cost or obligation. This added benefit alone could be worth far more than the cover price of your book!

You will find our e-mail address at the end of the book. But you really should read everything else first!

You are about to be reminded of things that you already know and also some things that are new to you. Just because we know how to do something, it does not follow that we do it. So ask yourself regularly, "Am I doing what I know I need to do today?"

Disclaimer Notice

This book offers business information and guidance only and is not intended as direct advice. I have no control over the way that you use the information contained within these pages – you alone are responsible for compliance with local rules and regulations, with governmental obligations and, equally importantly, for the outcomes of any actions that you take.

This book is a valuable guide and I recommend that you always employ qualified professional specialist advice. Remember, the responsibility for the way that you apply the information contained in this book is yours.

Chapter One

Now Review Now

Where you are now in relation to when you started?
Are you where you want to be?

Synopsis

This chapter is about soul-searching. If you have been doing your own thing for a year or more, it is important that you read this chapter now. The principles apply to every manufacturing, service or retail business. They apply to every professional practice. In short, unless you work for someone else or unless you are unemployed, they apply to you and your business. We begin with a brief but true story.

Although the shop was in a secondary shopping area, Julian felt that the savings on rent, compared with a prime site, would allow him to generate traffic by extensive local advertising.

He was in the insurance business. He had learned his trade as an employee within a big company and had built up an impressive list of contacts. Now he was ready to broker insurance on just about anything from cars to cats, from houses to horses and from freezers to floods.

His business boomed. So much so, that he became a victim of his own success. Within a year he had a staff of six. By reducing his commission he was able to offer extremely competitive rates, and word soon spread that this was the place to go for great deals.

However, Julian was not a well-organised man. The back office, where all the essential paperwork was done, was in a state of chaos. Files littered the desks and every available surface. Inevitably, mistakes were made. The staff became more and more stressed and, as a result, took increasingly frequent sick days. This added to the pressure, and mistakes occurred more often.

Soon his key man, Tom, could not take the situation any longer. He had been well rewarded for his work but felt that he just had to get off the treadmill. Using his recent experience and business network, Tom sought premises in the next town. He decided to start his own business, modelled on all that was good about Julian's company and with an added focus on avoiding that which Tom considered was bad.

Within a year Tom was drawing customers away from his former boss. One evening, he strolled past the shop where he had previously worked and immediately noticed that the fascia sign had two missing letters. The door, which always had a tendency to stick, had still not been repaired. Instead it bore a handwritten notice asking clients to 'push hard'. There was graffiti on the side of the building.

Peering through the dirty windows he noticed the display had not been changed since he left. Many of the 'special offer' posters were outdated, faded and peeling away from the walls. There was a collection of dead insects on the floor of the window, and one of the spotlights had failed and not been replaced. He noted that the toppling piles of paperwork had overflowed from the back office and now littered the counter.

Tom returned to his own spotless premises which reflected his own neat and orderly lifestyle. Instead of following the industry standard practice of rewarding his growing staff with ever greater percentages of commission, he offered them bonuses for every month in which they had no mistakes and generated no complaints.

Julian went out of business soon afterwards and told his friends and family that the fast growth of internet insurance was the cause of his company's failure. After a decent interval Tom acquired the premises. He now owns eight branches and the ninth is about to open.

The point of this story is that your business is a reflection of you. Its ethos, culture and public persona will be indelibly marked with your own sense of values, ethics and approaches to life.

If you are untidy, inefficient and disorganised then your business will soon be the same. If you are in a creative business where clients or customers do not visit your premises, you may think this is unimportant. Perhaps you always work at your clients' homes or businesses? In this case, you are very much the face of your business. They will pick up on your characteristics and will form a split-second decision about whether to hire you or not.

Here is a simple and revealing exercise called PACE, which stands for Personality, Attitude, Commitment and Excellence.

DIAGNOSTIC QUESTION BOX

What impression does your business face make?

The PACE Exercise

Decide right now on a time and place where you can be alone and quiet for as long as it takes, allowing at least half an hour. Focusing on yourself, rather than on your business, award yourself marks out of 10 for each statement. If you disagree absolutely, your mark should be 1. If you agree totally, give yourself 10. If you are unsure, then make an educated estimate between those two extremes.

Personality	**Total**
I am enthusiastic	_____
I have a positive attitude	_____
I make friends easily	_____
I lead a well-ordered life	_____
I am good at setting priorities	_____
I usually see the best in others	_____
I am honest	_____
I am ethical	_____
I admit my mistakes	_____

I give reasons rather than excuses   _____

I value my abilities   _____

I am ready, willing and able to improve myself   _____

I am not a moody person   _____

I have a good work/life balance   _____

My word is my bond   _____

I am fair   _____

I give praise where it is due   _____

I walk my talk   _____

Maximum possible score 180. Your score   _____

Attitude	**Total**
I am open to new ideas	_____
When something works well for me, I do more of the same	_____
When something isn't working, I change it	_____
I believe strongly in my own abilities	_____
I believe strongly in the abilities of others	_____
When I have gaps in my knowledge I am not afraid to seek assistance	_____
I have an extensive network of contacts that can help when needed	_____
I can resolve problems or disputes easily and amicably	_____
I can hold my ground when I am right, without upsetting others	_____
I am prepared to do myself, whatever I ask someone else to do	_____
I do it now and do not procrastinate	_____
Maximum possible score 110. Your score	_____

Commitment	**Total**
I am totally committed to my personal success	_____
I am totally committed to the success of my business	_____
I am committed to supporting my staff	_____
I am committed to the concept of constant improvement	_____

I pay my debts and dues on time and in full _____

I keep appointments punctually _____

I always 'go the extra mile' _____

I do whatever it takes _____

Maximum possible score 80. Your score _____

Excellence **Total**

My original business idea was good _____

My business today is pretty much as I envisaged it
back then _____

I generally under-promise and over-deliver _____

I believe there is always a better way _____

I honour my guarantees and promises _____

Only the best is good enough for me _____

Only the best is good enough for my clients _____

Maximum possible score 70. Your score _____

Well done on completing this exercise. This indicates that you have a willingness to listen, to follow instructions, to work on yourself and your business and to tap into the undeniable unused potential in both.

If you scored less than fifty per cent of the maximum scores in each category, you have some serious realignment to do and you will find the rest of this book absolutely essential. Look at each individual statement that scored 5 or less and ask yourself: "Am I willing to change this to gain a higher score?" If the answer is 'no', then what are your reasons for not wanting to change?

If the answer is 'yes', keep reading and return to the PACE exercise after you have read the rest of the book, and revisit your scores. Meanwhile, decide now on one single, simple positive step that you can take tomorrow in each category to raise those 5 or less scores. Every one of them!

As for the individual scores of 6 and above, do not be tempted to rest on your previous or current track record. Remember that ten years' experience is worthless if it is just one year's experience repeated ten times! There is still work to be done to ensure you stay in the top ranking.

Before the PACE exercise I said that your business is a reflection of you. That exercise should have given you insight into your strengths and any areas that need attention. It is almost certain, unless you have employees who compensate for the weak areas, that your business – whatever its size – will mirror these same traits.

The PACE activity is not about the formal business plans or marketing plans that you created to keep your bank manager or business adviser happy. It is about what went on inside your head when you created your business.

Why did you start it? List as many reasons as you can recall. Consider whether your main motivation was wealth generation, service, happiness, meeting a need, the empowerment of doing your own thing, pride, necessity or some other drive.

NEW Focus

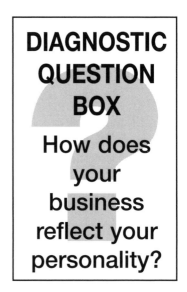

DIAGNOSTIC QUESTION BOX

How does your business reflect your personality?

Did you have a mental picture back then of how your business would look and function now? How does that model compare with the reality of now? Is 'now' better than your earlier vision or not as good? Maybe it has gone in a totally different direction?

If you could turn the clock back, what would you do differently? Why? What impact would the differences have made to your current business in terms of growth, return on financial and time investments, and work/life balance? Which one of the differences would have had the biggest impact or improvement with the smallest effort or investment?

I am not able to give you specific right or wrong answers because your individual circumstances are unique to you. I know that YOU instinctively know the answers which are right for you. That is the real value of this exercise. It encourages you to look for the answers that are within you.

Do you have a *job*, a *business* or a *practice*? Beware, because how you answer will reveal a great deal about your perception of self-value, and this perception will colour the way that your customers or clients think of your enterprise. That, in turn, will influence their decision to use your services or those of a competitor.

I asked three self-employed carpenters the same question about having a job, business or practice.

The first, dressed in clothing that looked as if it had come from the local charity shop and had not been washed for months, answered, 'a job'. "I do a good job and people recommend me to their friends. I work out a price for each job, I buy the materials for each job, I plan it and do what is needed. Then I get cash for the job and move on to the next one. My name is my reputation and I scrape a reasonable living."

The second carpenter, dressed in clean overalls with a logo on the breast pocket, replied, 'a business'. "I have a property renovation and repair business. It has a registered name and website that are both clearly displayed on the side of my van. It is VAT registered and I take pride in keeping my paperwork orderly."

The final carpenter wore a suit. "When people invite me into their home or business I believe that I am showing them courtesy and respect by being prompt and looking smart. I have a lifestyle practice that allows them to create the design effects they have seen on television or in glossy magazines. Of course, I provide dust sheets and wear a working uniform once I am on an assignment."

Three individuals with similar training, experience and trade skills – all that differentiated them was their attitude and the way they described what they did.

The one with a 'job' was treated as an inferior professional by the majority of his customers. He did not expect to be invited inside other than to see the customer's requirements. He did not expect to be paid much more than the national minimum wage because he thought that was all that most of his 'punters' could afford.

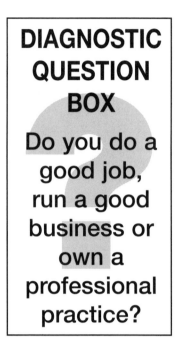

DIAGNOSTIC QUESTION BOX

Do you do a good job, run a good business or own a professional practice?

The one with a 'business' was usually invited inside through the back door of largely middle-class homes and was told when he was expected to arrive. He certainly earned respect and, because his potential clients liked his business-like attitude, they were happy to pay a premium price.

The one with a 'practice' called at the front door to keep appointments that he had made by telling the clients when *he* would be free to call. His clients were all in the upper-income bracket and expected to pay a high price for his specialist services. He saw to it that their expectations were met.

So, I ask again, regardless of your speciality, trade or expertise and, regardless of your enterprise, do you have a job, a business or a practice?

Why do you think this is? Are you happy with your answer? Of course, there is more to being in business than just creating a hefty bank balance, but do you have the right to deny yourself and your family the lifestyle that is within your reach by an upward change of attitude?

One of the most effective ways to acquire and sustain a positive attitude is to use the powerful mix of enthusiasm and motivation.

> *"Enthusiasm is the fuel that drives your motivation, but motivation is the engine that drives your business."*

True motivation can *only* come from within.

Self-motivation is fuelled by focus and enthusiasm. One without the other will not work. It is true that some short-lived motivation may come from outside sources, like attending a seminar, or like a boss or spouse saying, "*unless* you do this, then that will happen", or "*if* you do this, then I will do that," as they hold out the promise of some future benefit or reward.

These external inputs are like a donkey being persuaded to follow the driver's wishes with a carrot or stick. Donkeys learn fast. A stick need only be applied once and then a brief glimpse of it is enough to maintain forward momentum. A carrot, however, can be applied as often as necessary. It is worth remembering that a carrot is simply a short orange stick applied to the front instead of the rear. Someone or something else can motivate you briefly, but that level of motivation will not be strong enough to create a lasting change in you and your business.

Different triggers motivate all humans. However, there are three basic principles that apply to every person on this planet:

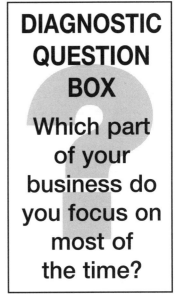

DIAGNOSTIC QUESTION BOX

Which part of your business do you focus on most of the time?

1. The only true and lasting motivation is self-motivation.

2. You are strongly motivated to meet your needs and less strongly motivated to meet your wants.

3. Self-motivation is powered by the prevention of pain and the pursuit of pleasure.

In the next chapter we will look at the aspect of focus in more detail as we explore the fascinating area of goals and their achievement. Firstly though, you need to examine your motivation because without it you stand less chance of achieving your personal and business goals.

Self-motivation means that you are doing something, like creating and running your business, because YOU want to, not because someone else wants you to. A suggestion from someone else might well be the catalyst that causes you to start a venture, so that you can meet a perceived need from potential clients, but it is essential that it is sustained by your own motivation and desire.

Every action that you take – without exception – produces a result or an outcome. Conversely, it follows that, if you focus strongly enough on your desired outcome, you will be strongly self-motivated to take whatever action is needed to achieve it.

Prevention of pain is a negative and powerful motivator. It kicks in when you realise that you need to take some action to avoid an uncomfortable situation from deteriorating further. For example, if you ignore a telephone bill you will eventually be disconnected, lose clients and incur a penalty fee. So, although it may be annoying and inconvenient to pay the bill, you are motivated to take the action to avoid an even greater pain and costly inconvenience.

The pursuit of pleasure is an equally powerful, but positive, motivator. I am sure that you can think of many examples from your own experience where you may have planned a holiday or an outing. You certainly did whatever was needed to ensure that it happened.

The pain that you seek to avoid does not need to be physical, like toothache. It is often more subtle and can be mental, as evidenced by high stress levels, depression or mood swings. Pursuit of pleasure does not have to mean a materialistic reward. It can be as simple as the great glow of satisfaction you experience when you know that you have done something extremely well.

As you develop your business, you will be somewhere along an imaginary railway line between a station called *Pain* at one end and another called *Pleasure* at the other. As you move away from pain you must head towards pleasure, for there are no branch lines or sidings. There is, however, a gap!

Initially, like the donkey and the stick, you will be strongly motivated to move rapidly away from pain. Then, as the pain diminishes with distance, it reduces your motivation so that you tend to slow down. Unless you have a very strong vision of your ultimate pleasure, that motivation can fall through the gap where it will diminish or disappear altogether. Then you will drift back towards the pain end of the track and the cycle repeats itself.

The way to sustain your forward momentum to cross the imaginary gap is, by constant repetition, to remind yourself of the pleasure at the end of the line. This will help you to keep positive, enthusiastic and focused.

Your question then is, "What is the ultimate pleasure that I can derive from running my business?"

If you are bored with your business, it may be, "How can I fill every moment of every day with meaningful activity?"

If you need extra funds, it may be, "How can I create sufficient money to meet my needs and my wants?"

Just for now, think of your own ultimate pleasure and write it down in your notebook or inspiration file so that you can refer to it later. In your notebook use colour, draw sketches, paste in photos – anything to remind you of your reasons for owning your own business.

Whenever you find yourself in the gap, ask yourself these simple questions:

Question	Answer
What is my level of motivation concerning my business right now? High/medium/low	_____
Is it OK if I increase that level of motivation?	_____
What will it take to increase my avoidance of pain and my desire for pleasure?	_____
Is it OK for me to take that action now?	_____
What action will that be?	_____
When will I take it?	_____

If your answer to any of these questions is, "I don't know" then the clincher question is, "If I did know, what do I think the answer *could* be?"

If you still don't know, here is the ultimate clincher question: "What additional information do I need to answer the question?"

Now, set goals to acquire that information. You will discover how to do this in the next chapter.

Personal and business success are inextricably intertwined. Here is a fundamental and basic truth concerning coaching and business success – you can only start from where you are now. What has gone before has gone. No amount of soul-searching, weeping or negative thinking can change it. You will have learned any lessons that you needed in order to grow, and now it is time to move on and forward.

If you attempt to drive a car with your attention focused mainly on the rear view mirror, you will miss the turnings of opportunity ahead of you and increase your chances of having a crash. Instead, drive with enthusiasm looking through a clear and spotless wind-screen into the future of your business. You CAN improve your business success – now have the courage, release your handbrake of real and imagined failure and jump into your business journey.

Get ready to plan the route to the next level on your business journey by reading Chapter 2!

Diagnostic Action Box

1. Make the mental picture of your ultimate pleasure as big, brash and bright as you can

2. Decide where you are going to focus your energies and attention over the next month

3. What does your business face say about you?

4. What is the ultimate pleasure that you can aim for from running your business?

5. What actions do you need to take right now to move your business forward?

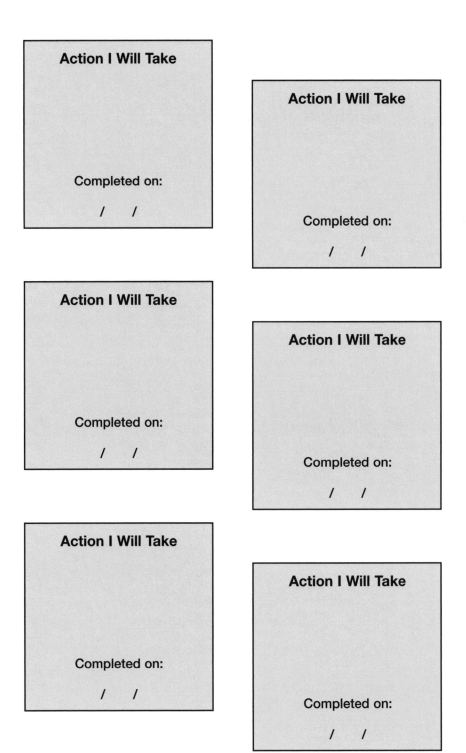

Action I Will Take

Completed on:

/   /

Action I Will Take

Completed on:

/   /

Action I Will Take

Completed on:

/   /

Action I Will Take

Completed on:

/   /

Action I Will Take

Completed on:

/   /

Action I Will Take

Completed on:

/   /

Chapter Two

The Secrets of Setting Goals

Be careful what you seek, because when you follow this system exactly –
you will get it!

Synopsis

This chapter concentrates on setting your personal and business goals. It offers a logical, practical and proven sequence of activities that allow you to convert any dream or idea into a goal. The opening true story is very short but it contains an incredibly important lesson.

Nigel thought he had a job for life when he landed a part in Britain's longest running television soap opera. Then, to boost viewing figures, the producer decided that his character would meet a gruesome and dramatic end.

At first Nigel welcomed the break from the punishing daily rehearsal and filming pattern. He still had a lifestyle that matched his former income but his savings quickly evaporated. To maintain his public image he borrowed and drifted ever deeper into debt. An avalanche of bills that he could not pay presented him with his wake-up call.

He remembered a book that another cast member had given him to read in his dressing room between takes. It was about goal setting. Without reference to the book, he decided there and then to set himself this goal: "Six months from today, I am totally debt-free."

Exactly six months later he was forced into bankruptcy. This is the ultimate debt-free state. He had achieved his goal, but it was not what he had in mind when he wrote it.

When you are setting your goals you must be careful and specific. Your subconscious mind will lead you powerfully towards your goals but it will not judge, edit out, interpret or waver. It does not ask how or why. Think of your unconscious mind as a heat-seeking missile; it just goes where it is pointed with single-minded determination. Keep this in mind as you work through this chapter.

It is time for me to reveal the six essential steps to help you avoid making errors similar to Nigel's when you set goals for your business and your personal life. The principles hold true whether you are preparing to launch your enterprise or if it is already up and running. They also apply to absolutely any business, large or small, public or private sector and any industry or service.

Six Step Goals

Step One: Know what you want

Carefully consider what you want. I know it sounds obvious, but you would be surprised how many business owners have never considered their 'wants' and have not written them down. If you were to ask the next five people that you meet, "What do you want your life to be?" or "What would you like to do?" expect at least four of them to immediately answer with what they don't want!

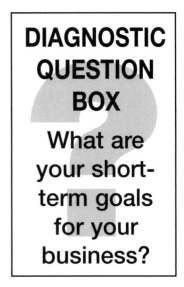

DIAGNOSTIC QUESTION BOX

What are your short-term goals for your business?

This simply means that they are more motivated by 'moving away from' than 'moving towards'. Remember the train in the gap between the stations of pain and pleasure – when you know what you do not want rather than what you do, you are still moving away from of pain. Fortunately, this can be a useful starting point. If it easier for you to consider what it is you do not want, define it clearly and, after you have completed this task, ponder the opposite – this generally becomes what you do want.

There is an ancient saying along the lines that for every desire there is always the means for its fulfilment. Just for now, it is okay to be brief, and to just use key words or short phrases to describe what you want.

You can write one line statements. Below is an extract from a list that was written by a young married couple who had a successful small shop. They worked together on this list over a period of one week. Eventually it ran to over fifty items.

> A new blind for the shop front
> New window display lights
> Another shop in the next town
> Reliable staff
> Better profit margins
> More customers
> More savings on deposit
> More time with the children

Start your own list and, if it helps, think of it as a wish-list. Once you have your first draft list, allow it to mature undisturbed for a week. When you return to it you will find that there are some things you didn't really want at all! Just draw a single line through them so that you can still read them later. At this stage you will probably have a few more items to add as well.

This refining stage continues by checking your remaining items to see if any of them cancel each other out. In the extract above, it immediately becomes obvious that another shop and more customers will result in less time with the children. Our couple decided that quality family time was more important to them than the other two items, so they simply decided to downgrade their priority for a while. *DEFINE WORKING HOURS/CASE LOAD/ APPOINTMENT TIMES (WEEKENDS!)*

To conclude this first step, put a priority tracking number by each item on your list. You can also rearrange the sequence so you can see in which order you want things to happen. This is only a wish-list. It does not become a goal-list until you have taken the remaining five steps.

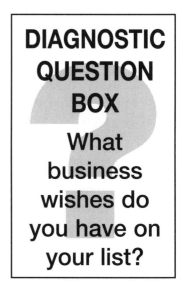

DIAGNOSTIC QUESTION BOX

What business wishes do you have on your list?

Step Two: Be specific

You will need a few sheets of paper for this step. At the top write your one line description from your wish-list. For the sake of demonstration, let us use the example of, "Another shop in the next town."

You will recall from the story at the start of this chapter that Nigel achieved his goal but not in the way he expected. He was not specific enough. The sorts of specific questions that our couple asked themselves were:

Name the next town?
Why there?
Which area of town?
Why there?
Which street?
Why there?
Rent or buy outright?
Leasehold or freehold?
Lock-up or with accommodation?
Live over or stay put in present home?
How big?
Double- or single-fronted?
Parking and loading facilities?
Stockroom size and access?

Again, this is only a small selection of the sort of questions the young couple worked with. The full list included considerations about the competition, other stores that would attract passing trade, possibility of vandalism, dominant socio-economic class of the area ... and more. It was immediately apparent that they really wanted a lock-up shop but, in their first choice of street, there were none, so, just as step one presented a couple of wishes that ruled each other out, this exercise forced them to examine their priorities again.

Now go back to your wish-list. Take each item, break it down to specific details and ask yourself specific questions, as in the example above.

The next phase is to turn your list of wishes into a positive and cogent statement. In our example, this became: "A rented, lock-up, single-fronted shop in Market Street, in Whistleton, with 500 square feet of selling space, a stockroom and a toilet."

To complete this step, take photographs, make copies of maps, sketches and any other visual aids that will help you to confirm and affirm your goal. I admit that this may appear to be a time-consuming process but it is actually easier to do than it is to describe. In fact, when you are doing it for your own business goals, you may well be surprised at how engrossed you become and how fast the time passes. No matter how long it takes, it will be worth it. After all, you are creating goals that will become your reality. In fact, you are creating your future life, which is very empowering.

Step Three: Set realistic deadlines

A goal is not a goal until it has a timescale. It is good to be optimistic, but it is even better to be realistic. When you consider the timescale for your own goals, build in a generous contingency factor. If you do not need it, you will be delighted when you achieve each stage ahead of schedule. If unavoidable delays occur, you will be prepared and they will not diminish your enthusiasm and motivation.

In this step, take each goal in turn and slot it into one of three categories: short-term, medium-term and long-term. In our shop example, short-term could mean 'within a month' (fit new window display lights), medium-term could be 'within 12 weeks' (recruit reliable staff) and long-term might be one or two years (another shop).

In your own business, the time periods may be much longer, depending on the size of your goals and the nature of your enterprise.

To return to our example, the earlier statement of intent can now have a timescale attached to it:

> "Within 12 months of today's date, acquire a rented, lock-up, single-fronted shop in Market Street, in Whistleton, with 500 square feet of selling space, a stockroom and a toilet."

When it comes to goal setting for successful achievement, your deadlines and timescales are the lifelines that keep your business on track.

DIAGNOSTIC QUESTION BOX

When do you want to reach your medium- and long-term goals?

Step Four: Establish milestones

You are on a journey. Any trip is easier when you have a method to check your progress. As a careful driver, I know that my motorway journeys at the speed limit will usually work out at an average of 60 mph for the entire journey, which means that when I read 'Bournemouth 30' on a signpost, I have 30 minutes to go.

Set milestones for your goals and give yourself a small reward as each is met and passed. This will keep your motivation in good order. Look forward to passing each one. Your milestones are simply means of keeping track so that you can make any small adjustments as they become necessary. If an aircraft or ship is just one degree off course during the journey, this will cause the aircraft or ship to miss its destination by many miles. That is why pilots and autopilots make frequent but small adjustments throughout the journey's progress.

Your goal milestones must have dates. The timeline for acquiring that shop in our example might be:

By [date]   Contact estate agents
By [date]   View premises
By [date]   Negotiate price
By [date]   Make offer
By [date]   Arrange finance

And so on ... until 'Start trading'

Without milestones, your progress will be encumbered by millstones!

Step Five: Gather resources

Your most important resources are your attitude, energy, enthusiasm, determination and motivation. These will positively influence other people who are involved in your goals and business projects. You need to have these qualities and keep them in abundance.

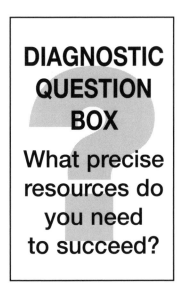

DIAGNOSTIC QUESTION BOX

What precise resources do you need to succeed?

It would be crazy to embark on a business in which you have no interest, so we must include interest as a resource. Experience is useful but can take time to acquire so, as you gain it, do not be ashamed to draw on the experiences of others to keep your forward momentum.

You will need the support of your family, friends and any business partners. You will need legal and accountancy input from appropriate professionals and, inevitably, you will need an awareness of government regulations and policies that surround most business ventures. You will need money too.

Consider one of your main goals and, using these examples as a guide, write your own list of resources and plan how you can acquire any that may be lacking. *During this goal setting phase, do not allow the lack of any of these resources to limit your vision. Avoid letting any perceived lack cause you to abandon your goal. Know what resources you want and concentrate on how you will acquire them. As their need arises, just trust that you WILL find the means – sometimes from the most unexpected sources.*

Step Six: Review and act

When you have completed these five steps, you are ready for the biggest one of all – the final step that brings it all together.

Review all your notes and thoughts about your goals. Summarise them into positive statements, each stated in the present tense and each with a timescale.

Tick off each item on your wish-list as you convert it into a written goal. To return to our example for the last time, you will recall that the wish-list item in step one was:

Another shop in the next town.

Then, in step two, it became:

A rented, lock-up, single-fronted shop in Market Street, in Whistleton, with 500 square feet of selling space, a stockroom and a toilet.

In step three it gained a deadline:

Within 12 months of today's date, acquire a rented, lock-up, single-fronted shop in Market Street, in Whistleton, with 500 square feet of selling space, a stockroom and a toilet.

Then our couple gave serious consideration to their milestones and resources. It is now time for the final wording:

IT IS NOW // AND I HAVE — — —

> *It is now (target date) and we have a rented, lock-up, single-fronted shop in Market Street, in Whistleton, with 500 square feet of selling space, a stockroom and a toilet.*

Do this for each of your goals. For some smaller short-term goals it will take just a couple of minutes (e.g. new window display lights). You may find that some larger goals will need to be broken down into a series of smaller ones. However, the same conditions and steps apply.

It is time for action. Write or draw each goal on a postcard in your neatest handwriting using as much colour as you can. Create a mental picture of what you will feel, see, hear, touch and smell when you achieve that goal. This is your mental rehearsal for the success that is coming. Keep your goal cards in your pocket, wallet or handbag where you can find them easily. Read them twice every day – for most of us, the best times are first thing each morning and last thing each night.

DIAGNOSTIC QUESTION BOX

How many written goals do you carry around with you every day?

Your conscious mind will find this constant repetition tedious and will want you to stop. You must override this tendency because the whole purpose is to feed your subconscious mind, which will guide all your actions towards achieving your goals.

Every action that you take, every thought that you have and every word that you say will then lead you towards your goals. If you fail to review your cards daily, those same actions will, at best, maintain the current situation or, at worst, move you away from your goals. Repetition is the key.

Each day, select your next significant action for each of your goals. Even if it is as small as cutting out a magazine article that could help you, do it! Then think about your next significant action. Monitor your progress against your milestones.

I make no apology for repeating the word 'action' so often here. If you do nothing, you will gain nothing. When you take a series of regular significant actions, you will achieve your goals.

Setting and achieving goals is not a one-off exercise for, as soon as you achieve one goal, you should be thinking about creating your next one. The more you achieve, the easier it becomes to continue achieving.

When you have followed all the steps in this chapter, you have just one more task. On the back of each goal postcard, write: "I will know that I have achieved this goal when ..." After all, there is little point in chasing a goal that is already a reality. Also, at the bottom of each card, write the reward you will give to yourself for this specific goal achievement. Have a variety of rewards to add fun and spice to the process.

I recommend that you return to this chapter regularly to revise what you are doing. If you find that you have slipped into the bad habit of taking short cuts, you can refocus and get back on track. Goal setting works; I have proven it in my own business. I have proven it in my personal life. My clients have proven it in their lives and businesses. Millions of people around the world have proven it.

Do it and prove it!

Diagnostic Action Box

1. Review your current situation

2. Work on your goal plan

3. Decide which of your goals has the highest priority

4. Do one thing now, towards your goal

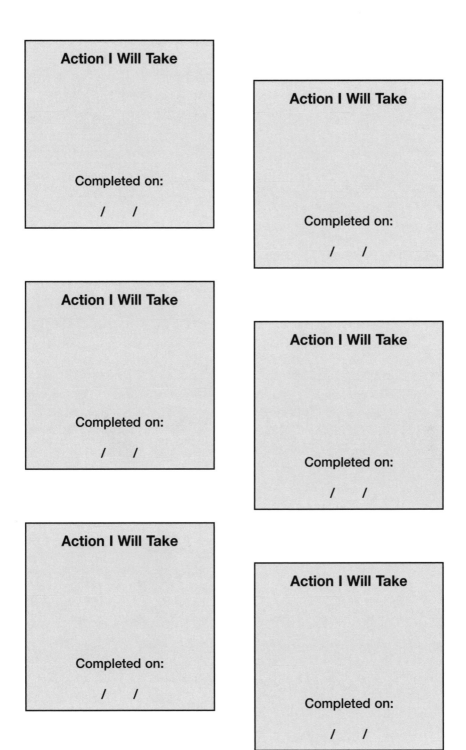

Chapter Three

Time Is Money

Now you have clear goals and know where you are going, you will need to manage your time effectively to get you there.

Synopsis

You know that time can equal money, and you probably think you already spend your time wisely, or perhaps you think that you do not have time to read this chapter? Do you want great ideas on how to find 'spare' time and how to use it? This is a must-read chapter for every small business owner – especially those who cannot find the time to read it!

Zoë was the owner of a very expensive and exclusive fashion shop. Her twin sister was unemployed and living on benefits. Zoë was also a magistrate, a local councillor, Chair of several charities, a leading light of her local amateur dramatic society and she had just launched a model agency business as her potential pension. It appeared that the more she did, the more time she had to devote to each interest and, as a result, she never seemed to be rushed and even had quality time to spend with her husband and children.

Her twin sister was constantly complaining about the lack of time as she drifted through each day, sometimes starting a domestic chore and becoming bored before it was finished. Then, feeling tired, she would watch a few hours of television. She could not understand how her sister managed to achieve so much.

Despite the vast gulf between their lifestyles, the women enjoyed a close relationship and would meet regularly at their favourite coffee shop. During one of these conversations, Zoë explained her concept of time to her sister. She told her "either use it or lose it". Then she went on to explain that, although we all have the same number of hours in the day, it is the *way* we use them that makes the difference.

> She invited her sister to describe, in some detail, what she would do tomorrow and the day after. This simple request presented some difficulties for her sister. With the aid of a pen and a paper napkin, they blocked out each two-hour period. Her sister thought about what they had discussed all the way home. By the time she got there, she had mentally planned every single hour of the next day for the first time in her life. To her surprise, instead of finding it a burden, she went to bed with excitement for the day ahead. Her journey to a focused future had begun.

Time is your most important commodity. There, I have said it. You cannot afford to waste any time because it is not refundable. You cannot mortgage it or borrow it from someone else. You are given the same amount every day and, at the end of the day, it has gone.

Everyone has the same amount, it is what you do with it that is the important part. I am not suggesting that you currently waste time deliberately; it's just that, as a business owner, you can easily become involved in the details and gradually create unhealthy processes, procedures and politics. These all absorb your time unproductively.

This valuable Diagnostic Time Chart may reveal how you lose momentum on time-wasting activities. I highly recommend that you invest some of your valuable time to complete the chart, as you may discover ways to use your time more productively.

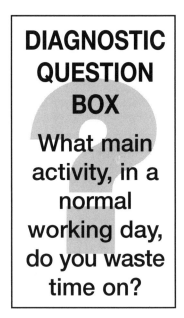

DIAGNOSTIC QUESTION BOX
What main activity, in a normal working day, do you waste time on?

Consider each statement and answer honestly. If it is true of you, or even partially true of you, put a tick in the box. As you go though the exercise you will begin to see a pattern of the time-taking tasks emerging and this will help you to take corrective and preventive action.

Diagnostic Time Chart

Telephone calls

☐ Discussions are unnecessarily long and directionless

☐ You want/need to be available to all outside calls
☐ No one to cover the calls for you

☐ Lack of priorities – all calls handled as they come in
☐ Unrealistic estimation of length of calls
☐ Calls becomes involved in details
☐ Uncontrolled conversations

Response in a crisis

☐ Lack of priorities
☐ Doing too many things = no direction of effort
☐ Lack of foresight. No idea of the outcomes of actions
☐ Treating small problems the same as a full crisis

☐ Overlooking any possible negative consequences

☐ Inability to say 'no'
☐ People assume you will say 'yes'

Decisions

☐ Addicted to details. Always need more information before you decide
☐ Irrational method for decisions – emotional
☐ Fear of mistakes making you look silly or costing you money
☐ Unrealistic deadlines
☐ Putting off the unpleasant decisions
☐ Lack of faith in your own decision process
☐ Lack of knowledge of final outcome

Delegation

☐ Little faith in the abilities of other people
☐ Control freak – need to feel in control
☐ Inadequate or unclear instructions/training/coaching
☐ Fear that others will do the job more efficiently or more effectively
☐ More comfortable doing than controlling direction of tasks
☐ You know you can do the job better and quicker
☐ Everyone else is overworked as well

(continued)

31

☐☐☐☐☐ ☐☐ ☐☐☐☐ ☐☐☐☐☐☐☐

- Unclear guidance or responsibility
- Unclear/inadequate job descriptions
- Staff have responsibility but no authority and feel put upon
- Your managers are indecisive
- Job descriptions which overlap

Power struggles in organisation
- Instructions unclear = poor performances
- No priorities

No job descriptions
- No time systems implemented
- Lack of self-discipline – easily distracted
- Would rather be doing instead of planning
- Thinking you have no time to plan

Inability to complete tasks
- Lack of deadlines given
- No respect for your own valuable time
- Overworked
- Unorganised work loads
- Not very inspired by certain jobs
- Lost your inspiration/motivation for company
- Carelessness on rushed jobs

☐☐☐☐☐ ☐☐ ☐☐☐☐ ☐☐☐☐☐☐☐

- You have no strategy for saying 'no'
- Wanting to help others regardless of self
- Wanting to feel important or needed
- Concern of being disliked for saying 'no'
- Ambition/desire to be seen to be busy

Over involved
- Wanting to be involved in everything
- Unsure of your priorities

Self discipline
- No performance standards to work towards
- No clear direction in your work or company
- Responding to the urgent instead of important
- Postponing the unpleasant tasks

Communication
- Staff misinterpret your instructions
- Difficulties interpreting your instructions
- No time deadlines set when giving tasks
- Recipient responds half-heartedly
- Delays in providing you with answers
- Over communication – too much information given
- Wrong media used to communicate, i.e. e-mails

Well done! You now know the areas that take precious time from your busy schedule.

There are many ways to deal with this knowledge. You could attend a time management course from the hundreds in the training market place. Some of the courses teach you how to manage your time, as well as supplying a time system to help you stay on track. Although these systems work really well for a number of people, they can cause grief and guilt for others. Only you can decide if one of these systems will work for you. You may choose to hire a business coach or management consultant to offer you help with your time control issues and to show you how to prioritise your work schedule. Time management is just another term for self management because, when you manage your time, you manage yourself.

The to-do list system is a favourite of many business owners and is very effective if used correctly, but it can become a stress accelerant if used incorrectly. The common mistake when using this system is to write a long list of things that need to be done during that day and then attempting to complete each task in the written sequence. The error is then compounded by adding new tasks to the end of the list, regardless of their importance or urgency. At the end of the day there are usually uncompleted tasks on the list. Think of the compounding negative impact and sense of failure when you reach every evening in the knowledge that you have not completed your to-do list!

In 1959, psychologist Frederick Herzberg published his book, *The Motivation to Work*. It included his Motivation-Hygiene Theory (the two factor theory) research. The second factor of this research, into 'human satisfiers or motivation', discovered that people are more motivated, and remain so for a longer period, when they feel a sense of achievement.

How can you ever feel a sense of achievement if, at the end of every day, you still have uncompleted tasks on your list? You not only feel the daily build up of stress caused by guilt about them, you also remove any sense of achievement you could feel about the tasks that you did do. In other words, by incorrect use of a to-do list, you destroy your long-term motivation and slowly but surely you lose heart and passion for your job or company.

The effective way of using a to-do list and maintaining motivation is by using a strategy based around priorities and goals.

The key to all good time management is to develop a clear set of goals or outcomes which you are passionate about attaining. Without goals you will struggle with time management.

We covered goal setting in the last chapter and you should now have a clear set of written outcomes to work towards. These will make your time management and decision making easier and faster.

DIAGNOSTIC QUESTION BOX

At the end of the day do you feel a sense of achievement or a feeling of overwhelm?

Three easy methods for using to-do lists effectively

Using lists can be an efficient strategy to ensure you know what you have to do, to act as a reminder to do the tasks and as a check and balance against failure to complete tasks.

Method A

Before you put a task on the list, ask yourself this: "If I do this task, will it take me closer to my goals?"

If the answer is 'yes', add it to the list. If the answer is 'no', leave it off.

Method B

Determine if the task falls into a priority category based on imme-diacy and importance to reaching your goals. Group tasks together into three separate priority categories:

1. Tasks which need immediate attention and *are* important to reaching your goals.
2. Tasks which are important, *need* to be done to reach your goals and *can* be done when time permits. These tasks need to have date stamps on them. With due dates noted, you will not over-look the importance and impact that an individual task may have on the overall goal strategy.
3. Tasks which need immediate attention and *are not* important to reaching your goals.

When a new task arises, determine whether it is a 1, 2, or 3 type. Write your allocated number next to the task and group it with the other tasks in that number.

Then, during the working day, you should concentrate on number 1 tasks first.

Every day, do at least one of the tasks on the number 2 tasks list.

With all the number 3 tasks, decide to delegate or postpone action according to the impact this will have on your business or your long-term goals. The time involved in doing this type of task may be one of your deciding factors.

Method C

This method involves using two separate lists simultaneously:

- List A contains a maximum of ten tasks and should be written the night before.
- List B contains all the tasks you have to do this week/month.

You work exclusively on List A during the day. When these tasks are completed, you reward yourself by cherry picking (selecting the tasks you like doing) from List B.

At the end of the day, if you have completed all your List A tasks, you will feel a sense of achievement and will have met the top Herzberg motivation factor. Using this method will help you to stay motivated for longer.

If, however, a task comes to you which is urgent and needs immediate action put it on List A and move another task from List A to List B. This is very important. You must strictly discipline yourself to limiting List A to a maximum of ten tasks, otherwise you will simply revert to a long list and a feeling of overwhelm. Control your lists.

DIAGNOSTIC QUESTION BOX

Would using an alarm clock or alarm system help you to manage your time into effective, focused activity slots?

Actions to defeat time-takers

Consider these time-takers and the actions you can take to defeat them.

Identify your top five time-takers from the diagnostic time chart on the opposite page (activities where your time investment is higher or disproportionate to your results) and implement the suggested action. If it works for you, keep on doing it. If you do not get the result you are looking for, you will have started a process of change which will produce the answer that is right for you. Be your own time police by keeping track of your time-takers. When you find them, lock them up and throw away the key!

Time Reclaim Chart

CAUSES OF TIME-TAKERS	ACTIONS TO TAKE BACK TIME
Telephone calls	**Actions**
Discussions are unnecessarily long and directionless	Plan your outcomes before the call and use a timer
You want/need to be available to all outside calls	Delegate to staff or outsource all calls to a professional call centre
No one to cover the calls for you	Outsource all calls to a professional call centre
Lack of priorities – all calls handled as they come in	Decide on time blocks to deal with the calls and delegate call answering
Unrealistic estimation of length of call	Decide on your outcome for the call at the beginning and as soon as you have reached it – close the call
Call becomes involved in details	Ask caller to send you an e-mail – this allows you to select the time to look at the details
Uncontrolled conversations	Control them now!
Over-involved	**Actions**
Wanting to be involved in everything	Ask for end of day reviews and let go!
Unsure of your priorities	Check time control chart
Underestimating job completion times	Keep records and over-estimate time tasks will take
Overwhelming pressure of paper piles	Clear your decks and file immediately. Use the one touch rule
Decisions	**Actions**
Addicted to details	Decide on a date and time when the decision will be made, regardless of information received
Irrational method for decisions – emotional	Use a matrix system to decide
Fear of mistakes making you look silly or costing you money	Failure is only feedback which you can use to aid successes

(continued)

37

Decisions (*continued*)
Unrealistic deadlines
Putting off unpleasant decisions
Lack of faith in your own decision process
Lack of knowledge of final outcome

Actions
Set deadlines based on previous information or expert advice
Do it now! Use a matrix
Use a coach or mentor
Determine the risk factor in making the decision

Response in a crisis
Lack of priorities
Doing too many things = no direction of effort
Lack of foresight – no thought to outcome of actions
Treating small problems the same as a full crisis

Overlooking any possible negative consequences
Inability to say 'no'
People assume you will say 'yes'
You have no strategy for saying 'no'
Wanting to help others regardless of self

Wanting to feel important or needed
Concern of being disliked for saying 'no'
Ambition/desire to be seen to be busy

Actions
Use time control chart
Use time control chart
Keep records and consider challenges when planning
Before taking action, ask yourself: "What would happen if I did nothing?"
Plan for all contingencies
You have a choice. Start saying 'no' to small issues – for practice
Decide to change this assumption
Say 'no' and follow it with alternative actions for the requester
Be very clear on your own outcomes/goals. Ask yourself: "Will this take me nearer to my goals?"
Ask yourself: "Am I doing this just to feel important or needed?"
Think of someone you like who says 'no'
You will be truly busy if you have clear goals

Delegation
Little faith in the abilities of your staff
Control freak – need to feel in control
Inadequate – unclear instructions/training/coaching

Fearing others will do the job more efficiently or more effectively

Actions
Take time to train and coach staff properly
Start by letting go of small unimportant tasks
Write a training plan for all the important tasks to which both parties can refer
Let them do it and spend your time working towards your goals

(continued)

Delegation (continued)

More comfortable doing than controlling direction of tasks

You know you can do the job better and quicker

Everyone else is overworked as well

Unclear guidance or responsibility

Unclear or inadequate job descriptions

Staff have responsibility but no authority and feel put upon

Your managers are indecisive

Job descriptions which overlap

Power struggles or distrust in organisation

Instructions unclear = poor performances

No priorities

No job descriptions

No time systems implemented

Lack of self-discipline – easily distracted

Would rather be doing instead of planning

Thinking you have no time to plan

Communication

Staff misinterpret your instructions

Difficulties interpreting your instructions

No time deadlines set when giving tasks

Actions

Train staff properly and you will be comfortable letting go

What will happen if you continue with this action?
Will doing this task take you closer to your goals?
Ask for clear instructions and information about expected outcomes

Write them now. Get staff to edit the job descriptions to include all tasks

Start giving small amounts of authority until you are confident in the staff

Train them on the matrix process

Get staff to edit the job descriptions to include all tasks – then review and rewrite the descriptions

Start being honest and open – no favourites

Decide exactly what you expect and write it down

Use time control chart

Write them

Start one

Close office door at least once a day or if in open plan office use busy signs system

Employ a planner and agree to stick to the plans

Use the time control chart

Actions

Decide your outcome before speaking and write it down if necessary

Ask them to explain to you their understanding of what you said

Start setting deadlines – ask them how long they think it will take

(continued)

39

Communication (*continued*)
Recipient responds half-heartedly
Delays in providing you with answers

Over communication – too much information given
Wrong media used to communicate, i.e. e-mails

Actions
Ask them what it is they are not happy about
Always follow up five minutes after time has passed – this will set a pattern
Use instruction cards
Where possible speak directly to staff and ask for confirmation of understanding – see above

Inability to complete tasks
Lack of deadlines given
No respect for your own valuable time

Overworked

Unorganised work loads
Not very inspired by certain jobs
Lost your inspiration/motivation for company

Actions
State deadlines
Be very clear on your own outcomes/goals. Ask yourself: "Will this take me nearer to my goals?"
Before each task consider if there is anyone else who is able do this – delegate or outsource
Use time control charts
Remind yourself of the your long-term goals for inspiration
Remind yourself of your reason for starting the company and your long-term goals

Self discipline
No performance standards to work towards
Postponing unpleasant tasks
Responding to the urgent not the important

No clear direction in your work or company
Carelessness on rushed jobs

Actions
Set standards
Remind yourself of your long-term goals for inspiration
Be very clear on your own outcomes/goals. Ask yourself: "Will this take me nearer to my goals?"
Be very clear on your own outcomes/goals
Ask yourself: "If I have to do this again – what are the costs involved?"

Fundamentals for Efficient Management of Your Business Time

Acknowledge when you are not managing your time

How do you experience time? You can manage your time more effectively when you understand that it is your experience-based perception and not the actual physical flowing of time that affects your attitudes and understanding of time.

Are you aware of your surroundings and the people that you interact with when you feel time pressured – or do you just react?

Know exactly how much it is costing you

When you have a clear perception of physical time and combine this with its cost, you will regain control with a positive impact on your performance and that of your staff.

Work better, not harder

Plan your day the night before and put similar jobs together in a time block. Then work exclusively on these jobs during that time block.

Use travelling time to dictate or draft your letters or reports on a speech-operated recording device.

Make telephone calls (use safe, hands-free systems) which require no written action from you. Listen to motivational or personal development material. If you travel by train, replace the newspaper with business growth reading materials, or plan the outcome-focused agenda of your next meeting.

Time-blocking

Once you have a task list for the next day, group similar tasks together and allocate a time frame to do them. For example, telephone calls you have to make, or paperwork and e-mails you have to send. Be strict with yourself, ignore 'you have a new message' and only deal with e-mails during their allocated time slot.

Two useful tips:

1. Do not deal with e-mail as the first task of the day. It will take longer than you anticipate and throw your time-blocking system into disarray.
2. Use an alarm clock to keep you to your time slots. Set the alarm at the beginning of a task and as soon as the alarm sounds, stop the task and move on!

Prioritise your tasks

Distinguish between tasks which are important and tasks which are urgent. Consistently working on tasks which are important, but not necessarily urgent, will avoid the need to fire-fight those which eventually acquire urgency. This will increase your effectiveness.

Simplify

Simplify your environment, processes, procedures, marketing, communications and any aspect of your business. Clear clutter from all business spaces and follow a clear-desk policy for each evening.

Use the One Touch Method to deal with everything only once. This means that if you pick up a document or open an e-mail, you deal with it. Yes, deal with it to the point where you will not need to touch it again. When you touch the document you have three options:

1. Respond
2. Request more information
3. Rip up

If you use the One Touch Method in conjunction with a time-blocking system you will achieve more with less time.

Destroy distractions

Distractions are the devil to deal with, and create devilish deeds within your company.

Be clear about your daily outcomes and time plans and guard them with your life.

It is tempting to allow yourself to be distracted by events, staff, family, e-mails, telephone and so on. If you allow yourself to become distracted, you will never achieve your goals within the time frames you set.

Using a time-blocking process and sticking to it gives you a structure to

DIAGNOSTIC QUESTION BOX

Is this task money generating or cost generating?

work with. When time-blocking include periods to deal with distractions and make everyone aware that they can contact you then. This will help you to say, "No, I cannot deal with it now. I have a time slot which is ... and I will deal with it then."

You will become efficient and confident when you use a time-blocking system. You need to decide that you cannot do everything and, to be successful, you can choose to spend time on achieving your goals by deciding what price you will pay in time or short-term gratification. Successful people know they have to make sacrifices and give up things (or at least put them on hold until later) to get what they truly want. Remind yourself of your exact goals every day and exactly what you are prepared to give up in order to achieve them.

Manage meetings

The challenge with meetings is the time they take in relation to the results they deliver.

Always have an agenda, even if you have called an impromptu meeting. Write the reason for the meeting and the outcome you are looking to achieve on a board. Agree and keep to a timetable. Look at the items to discuss and determine exactly how much time each item will be given within the total time allocated for the whole meeting.

Never allow your agenda to have 'any other business'. It gives disgruntled attendees a platform and is absolutely unnecessary if everyone is prepared with all the information they need before they attend the meeting.

Keep meetings brief. Wherever possible have them in a space with no chairs; standing focuses the mind and reduces pointless discussions. Set ground rules – everyone contributes and has x minutes each to put forward their contribution without interruptions. Keep to the timetable and move any items not concluded to the next meeting.

Delegate or outsource

Think about any unnecessary tasks or those that can be done by someone else. Delegate these immediately.

How do you do it? First, write down every detail of the task in chronological order, select the best person for the task, spend time to train them properly, then simply delegate and let go. If you have no one to delegate to, there are companies providing a huge variety of soft skill services from answering the phone to bookkeeping. See Chapter 16, Outsourcing, for more information on this.

Do research on the providers, selecting the most appropriate one for your needs. Once selected, outsource specific tasks – the tasks which take too much of your time and can be outsourced with little impact on your profits and huge impact on your released time.

Busy signs system

Use this system with time blocking for best results. It imposes strict rules which all participants need to adhere to and is especially useful for open plan offices.

This is a visual system. Everyone who needs it for performance enhancement is allocated uninterruptible time slots (they need not all be the same length and not everybody may need uninterruptible time). The uninterruptible time slots are displayed for everyone in the company to see. A bold visual object or symbol is used to indicate that the person is in his/her uninterruptible time slot, and it is placed so that people approaching can be easily reminded not to interrupt.

A desk flag, a coloured cap or a coloured piece of fabric can be used to great effect. The single most important rule, on which this whole system rests, is that when the visual object or symbol is on display, the person *must not* be interrupted. Not even by you! Respect and follow the rules, and this system reduces distractions, maintains chains of thought, improves productivity and enables the company to significantly reduce the stress levels of all involved.

Time control chart

This chart (overleaf) will help you to devote your time to achieving your goals instead of spending time on unnecessary tasks. Use this chart as your to-do list and then mark each task between 1 to 10, with 1 being a low importance and 10 being highest importance. You can use weighting on individual tasks to add extra importance. Total each column and work on the highest scoring numbers first.

Remember if you are not working towards your own goals, you will most probably be working on somebody else's goals.

Time control chart

Task/job/meeting/ telephone call	Impact on sales if not done	Time to do	Urgent	Cost implication if not done	General impact	Totals

Cost your time

It is important to know exactly how much your time costs. This way you can make informed decisions on who is best placed to do the less skilled tasks.

How to cost time

Below is a simple formula which will enable you to evaluate the cost of your time and the cost of the time of each of your employees.

Annual salary	£
Bonus/commissions/dividends	£
+ 20% to cover pensions, NI, etc.	£
+ 80% basic salary (covers overheads, lighting, phone, heat, travel, admin, etc.)	£
Total	£
Divide total by 230 (average working days per year)	£
Divide result by average numbers hours worked each day	£
Total cost per hour	£

Once you understand how much your time costs, ask yourself, "Is this task good value for my time, or could it be more economical to outsource or delegate it?" It is easier to decide once you know how much it will cost you to do the task and how much it would cost a member of staff or an outsourcing company.

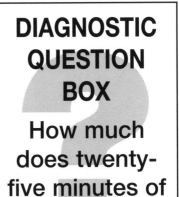

DIAGNOSTIC QUESTION BOX

How much does twenty-five minutes of your time actually cost?

Saving time with people

Do you do everything in your business? How many customers can you serve, telephones calls can you answer? With more people, you can achieve more than you can on your own. You can employ people, hire them on a temporary basis or use an outsourcing company. Identify the tasks that can be performed by other people. Then consider the costs and risks involved in employing or outsourcing and take action immediately. Your hours saved can be used to leverage other parts of the business!

Saving time with systems

Effective systems can save you time and money. Put a system into place for all or most routine and repeat tasks. It is usually more cost-effective to put a system in place rather than employing extra people. It is possible to systemise about seventy to eighty per cent of any business and it is worth taking time to do this. If you lack the necessary knowledge or skills, outsource the systemising!

Spend quality time on you!

Finally, remember to spend some time with your family, doing some healthy exercise, being with friends, in quiet reflection or meditation, on hobbies and having fun!

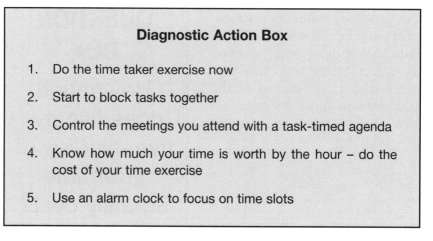

Diagnostic Action Box

1. Do the time taker exercise now

2. Start to block tasks together

3. Control the meetings you attend with a task-timed agenda

4. Know how much your time is worth by the hour – do the cost of your time exercise

5. Use an alarm clock to focus on time slots

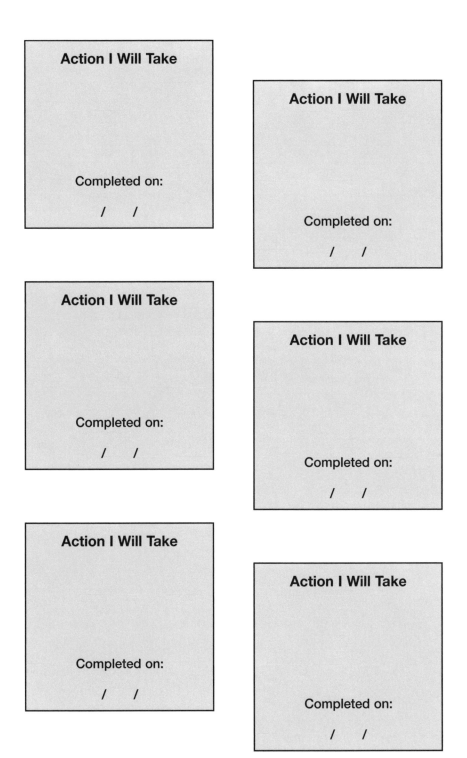

Chapter Four

Typical Customer Profile

Profiling your typical customers allows you to understand their needs and target those needs effectively.

Synopsis

This chapter looks at why it is important to define in as many ways as possible your typical customer. This knowledge will increase your sales and your return on promotional investments. Avoid being the 'average Joe' who simply promotes to everyone believing that their customer will work it out! YOU work it out, be very clear and target your market to get maximum returns.

Broadstairs is a small seaside resort town on the Kent coast. It is midway between its two brasher and bigger neighbours, Margate and Ramsgate. Because it has remained largely unspoilt over the years, Broadstairs has become the chosen retirement location for many Londoners.

Colin and Ruth Moorey looked for a shop to purchase in the town. They found a small wool, crafts and baby-wear business which seemed to have a great and under-utilised potential. Their thinking was along the lines of recognising that knitting was a pastime mainly enjoyed by more mature ladies, who would either knit clothes for their grandchildren or who would be ready, willing and able to buy designer brands of ready-made infant apparel.

The whole ambience of the shop, from window displays to counter and fittings, was firmly aimed at this traditional market. Within a few months they had doubled the turnover of the shop's previous owner, but it still failed to deliver the returns and profits they believed were possible.

Recognising the need to significantly expand their customer base, Colin spent several days observing the 'footfall' of passers-by while Ruth managed the store. He soon calculated that teenage girls formed the highest percentage, mostly because this shop was on the primary route from the nearby technical college to the town's cafes, chippies and sandwich shops. It was time for a rethink.

The problem seemed to be that their original customer base of knitters was declining as the elderly ladies either passed on or suffered failing eyesight and dexterity. When the focus shifted from elderly ladies to teenage girls, the business took off like a rocket. Our couple redecorated the store to appeal to the younger end of the market and they started evening classes (which were promoted in the college) to introduce youngsters to the world of knitting.

Although Colin never gained proficiency with needles, he acquired exclusive territory rights for a newly introduced Japanese knitting machine which he demonstrated with flair. They created an annual 'young knitter of the year' competition and gained extensive local and national press coverage. It took several months, but the shop was eventually turning over ten times the weekly trade of the previous owners and, by word of mouth recommendation, drew customers from the nearby towns too. All it took was a slight shift of focus about their 'typical' customer base.

You can have the best premises, products or services in the world. Unless people know that you exist and are open for trade, this is all you will have – no customers or clients, no sales, no profits and, very soon, no business.

To begin with, answer this simple question: "Which customers do you want to attract?" If you answered 'everyone', then you are destined to attract very few. Imagine for a moment you are using a hose to water your garden on a summer evening. With the 'everyone' mentality you will be using a fine oscillating spray, so that some droplets will hit a plant and an equal number will fall on bare earth. If you use a directed jet 100 per cent of your water will land on your target plants. Before you can even attempt any efforts at marketing, advertising and public relations, you must have a clear picture of your 'typical customer'. Only then do you have sufficient knowledge to reach them and address them effectively.

To take an extreme example, it would clearly be a complete waste of time and money to advertise high-priced computers in a magazine that is read by low-income manual workers, or to advertise heaters in a hot climate. Now you could be saying to yourself, "I would not be that ridiculous, it is obvious they would not be interested in my product." However, the interesting point is that often people market their products ineffectively due to the 'oscillating spray' technique. One of the main reasons for this could be money related. It is generally cheaper, for example, to put an advertisement in a local newspaper in preference to a closely targeted magazine or trade journal.

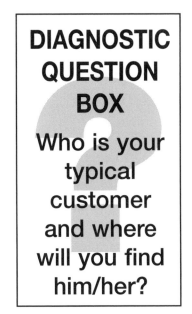

DIAGNOSTIC QUESTION BOX

Who is your typical customer and where will you find him/her?

If you have a business that offers more than one product or service, you may need to answer these questions for each product or service, or at least for each group of related items. The suggestions in brackets are not exclusive, so add any other categories that occur to you.

- Is your typical customer male, female or from both sex groups?
- What age group does your typical customer fall into? (Child, teenager, young adult, middle-aged, retired)
- What is your typical customer's disposable income group? (Poor, below average, average, above average, wealthy)
- What is the status grouping of your typical customer? (Unemployed, artisan, professional, employed, self-employed, manager, director, independent means)

Once you have answers to these questions – and it is a good idea to write them down – you now have a basic framework which you can use as a starting point for promoting your business. But you cannot begin yet, because you need more information.

Taking your typical customer basic framework, start to determine more specific details by answering these questions:

DIAGNOSTIC QUESTION BOX

What do I know about my typical customer?

- Where does your typical customer live? (Type of house, village, town, city, major metropolis, overseas country)
- Where does your typical customer work? (Office, factory, open air, retail, driving, home, hospital)
- Where does your typical customer go for leisure? (Clubs, restaurants, bars, coffee houses, gyms)
- What are the hobbies and interests of your typical customer? (Equestrian, sport, television, music, theatre)
- What does your typical customer read? (Magazine titles, newspaper titles, book categories)
- What does your typical customer listen to? (Pop music, classics, talk radio, iPods/MP3 players, podcasts, CDs)

I could fill the rest of this book with further examples but by now you should have the idea. Once you have the clearest possible typical customer picture you can begin to plan your promotions, starting with allocating the time that you need to invest. There is an often repeated adage in personal development circles that 'the map is not the territory'. This simply means that you can look at any map but it is only when you travel the route that you know the reality.

Take a trip to the places inhabited by your typical customer. Have a look at their work and leisure environments, go where they go, read what they read, listen to their type of music. You may feel like a private detective, but the purpose of your investigation is to get into your typical customer mindset.

The more you know about your typical customer, the better your target aim and the returns on your marketing, advertising and public relations investment. If you know some of the challenges and problems which beset your typical customer you can aim your marketing to solve the problems or to ease them, thus doing two things at once. First, you show the customer you know who they are and the issues that concern them. Second, you care enough to find solutions for them.

Within the context of this chapter, marketing encompasses all that you do to inspire and prolong a demand for your products or services. Here, advertising will make potential clients aware that you are the perfect business to fill that demand. Publicity is what other people might write or might say about you, and public relations (PR) is what you say, write or broadcast about your business.

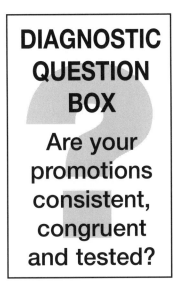

DIAGNOSTIC QUESTION BOX

Are your promotions consistent, congruent and tested?

Although marketing, advertising and public relations can be identified as separate topics, in truth, there are grey areas where they can overlap. I recommend you think of the three topics as layers that make up your promotional cake.

Three things to remember with your promotions

Consistency, Congruency and Testing.

Consistency

This simply means that anything and everything seen by your typical customer before, during and after their contact with your business *must* be consistent. If you constantly target your typical customer with a consistent message of understanding and as a provider of solutions, your name will become synonymous with their needs.

Congruency

Your promotional material must be congruent with traditional expectations or market expectations. If you manufacture clothes for babies, your typical customer will expect to see blue for boys and pink for girls. This will meet the majority of customers' expectations. The exception is if you are targeting a niche market of parents who want their children to look different, and you will know this because you have profiled your typical customer.

You must be prepared and able to deliver on all your claims and promises. A great idea is to plan to keep a little bit back (service or product) to enable you and your staff to over-deliver and thus exceed your typical customer's expectations. An example of this is to state 28-day delivery and manage 20-day delivery. *It is always better to under-promise and over-deliver!*

Let consistency and congruency flow over, around and through your business and allow them to permeate the minds of your customers.

Testing

To test your results you must clearly have some means of identifying which promotions worked for you. This is simply done and you will discover how when you get to Chapter 8, The Art of Advertising. Successful marketers and advertisers know the truth of 'test, test and test again'.

Typical customer public relations

Target your press releases and all your public relations to your typical customer. All press releases should be placed in publications your typical customer will read. All activities should be arranged in areas, time frames, styles and approaches that your typical customer will identify with. They should think: "This is for me, so I will attend" or "This is for me, so I will read the whole article."

Check your local directories and Yellow Pages. A tip is to start your PR activities locally – to test their effectiveness. If you have a niche, start in the most popular publication or venue. If you are consistently thinking of your typical customer's world, you will have a greater return on your investments.

Remember, it is important to define your typical customer completely if you are concerned about increasing your sales and your return on promotional investments. Avoid being the 'average Joe' who simply promotes to everyone and be very clear to target your market to get maximum returns.

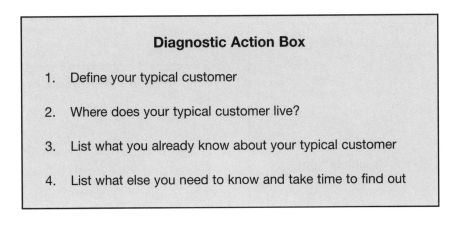

Diagnostic Action Box

1. Define your typical customer

2. Where does your typical customer live?

3. List what you already know about your typical customer

4. List what else you need to know and take time to find out

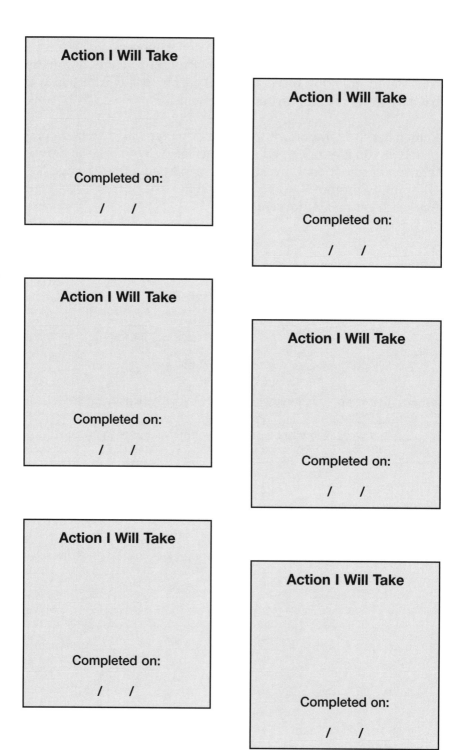

Chapter Five

From Lead to Sale

You have defined your ideal customer and have accurately targeted your marketing and publicity. Now on to the big step of creating the sales.

Synopsis

You might be tempted to skip this chapter in the belief that you know all about 'cold leads', 'referrals' and all the standard textbook stuff. That would be a shame because how you classify your lead will determine how you follow it up, and how you follow it up can be the difference between a sale made and a lost chance.

There was a company which made log cabins. To many prospective buyers they were simply 'sheds with attitude' but to the company founder Roger Bath, who was also the designer, every one was a miniature house. It had taken years of research, trial and error to create his range of cabins.

The prototype cabin was designed through the comparatively simple exercise of converting Roger's concept into drawings and then building it. The first buildings were dismantled to see what modifications would be needed to create a prefabricated flat-pack. This necessitated several alterations, but Roger was careful to ensure they would not compromise the integrity and durability of his designs. Yet more changes were needed to allow the components to be securely contained on standard wooden pallets for delivery to customers.

By now the original retail price had gone through the roof. So it was back to the drawing board for a cost reduction programme. By standardising custom parts and applying cost engineering concepts, the product range was ready to launch into the top end of the market.

As the publicity programme was rolled out, Roger recruited two salesmen.

Tony was the first. Although he had no previous sales experience, he had been involved with the company since the earliest days when he had helped to source the raw materials. He knew the product inside out – literally! He followed up every lead as soon as he could and allowed his product knowledge and enthusiasm to do the selling for him. Customers chose to buy as opposed to feeling that they had been sold to.

George was the other recruit. He would tell anyone who would listen that he was a 'born salesman' who could 'sell snow to the Eskimos'. He had sold encyclopaedias and vacuum cleaners door-to-door; he had sold double-glazing, loft insulation and even stone cladding when it was fashionable. George would group his leads around his busy social life and get to them 'as and when'. Then, he delivered such a hard sell that many seriously interested prospects were turned off.

The leads and enquiries were evenly distributed to both salesmen. Within the first six months Tony, the 'non-salesman', had outsold George by a ratio of four to one.

George left in a huff, blaming everyone but himself for his dismal results. Tony, who had an instinctive understanding of lead conversion, is still with the company and is enjoying a good income with profit-sharing incentives.

Very few people truly enjoy selling and yet it is the key to any successful business. No cash comes in until your product or service is sold. Whether you like it or not, this is a fact of business life. Previous chapters have described strategies and techniques for getting enquiries from genuinely interested potential customers who are ready, willing and able to buy from you. You have already converted them from 'suspects' – the entire population of your catchment demographic or chosen reservoir of potential customers – to 'prospects', those who have a need that you can satisfy.

At this stage your prospects are simply leads. Figuratively speaking, you have told them that you are open for business and they have checked you out. You are about to discover the next step, where you convert leads into selling appointments, telephoned orders or mailed-in orders with payment.

Not all of your leads are equal. Some are 'warm', for example, where personal recommendation has led them to you, and others are 'cold', where an individual has clicked the box on your website for more information or has responded to your advertisement out of curiosity.

If you are new to sales jargon, let me give you some examples of 'warm' and 'cold'. But first, how about 'red hot' leads?

Some years ago, I was involved with a training organisation that held free introductory seminars. Their objective was to attract potential students who would pay £2,000 to sign up for a distance learning course. The seminar presenters were professional communicators who created a storm of enthusiasm and audience participation. Although a few delegates left as soon as the presentations ended, most stopped by the many tables to buy the books and audio programmes that had been raved about during the presentation, and some wanted to qualify for the 'Sign up tonight and save twenty per cent' offer.

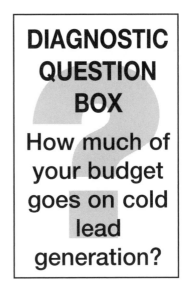

DIAGNOSTIC QUESTION BOX

How much of your budget goes on cold lead generation?

Within two hours, several hundred 'suspects' who walked through the door had been converted to 'prospects'. Then, while they were caught up in the dynamic excitement of the event, well over fifty per cent became 'buyers' – all within 120 minutes. They were 'red hot' leads!

You need to exercise some caution when dealing with red hot leads because you can get a bad burn if you expect every one of them to actually follow through. When the euphoria of the day fades, when they return to their real world and, probably, when that month's credit card bills arrive on their doorstep, they may well exercise their option to cancel within the cooling off period that you must legally offer. These people are known as having buyer's remorse. In the above example, the training organisation modified its approach slightly. Instead of making their evening free to all, they introduced a £25 charge which would be offset against the price of the course for those who signed up. This reduced 'red hot' enthusiasts to 'good and hot' people who had, effectively, pre-selected themselves as willing to pay for the information.

At the other end of the warmth scale, you have leads that are so cold they should be kept in the freezer. Think of the student hired to hand out fliers in the high street for a new gymnasium. He would achieve his objective when he had handed out 1000 fliers so, of course, he was indiscriminate and thrust one into the hands of everyone who walked past. These 'leads' were not even worthy of the name.

They are in the same category as the doorstep salesman who collects the names and addresses of people who have 'expressed an interest' simply so that they can get rid of him and return to whatever they were doing. In each instance the promoter is playing the numbers game. The strategy is based on the statistics which state there will be a one per cent response rate with this type of cold selling, and that one per cent of those who responded will be converted into a sale. Therefore, you need to expose a massive number of people to your sales message to derive any sales. It does not matter how many of these cold leads you collect, they will not spontaneously combust into heat! Just like frozen food tightly packed into a freezer, they will remain resolutely cold.

Some replacement window firms have grown big by starting with such techniques but, once they have gained an initial momentum, they have moved on to warm lead harvesting to grow huge.

Typical warm leads are people who have responded to your exhibition stand, advertisement or website. By taking a simple action, they have pre-qualified themselves as having an interest in your product or service. Even warmer are those who have been recommended to contact you by one of their trusted friends. That is why it is so important to ask every customer for referrals at the point when you deliver their goods.

With referrals, it is rare for anyone to volunteer the contact details of acquaintances who may be interested; you have to ask for them! If you ask for one, you may get none and your client may feel awkward that they were unable to respond to your request. Ask for five, and the chances are that they will come up with at least two. To encourage referrals, some companies offer a discount to their customers on their next order for each name provided.

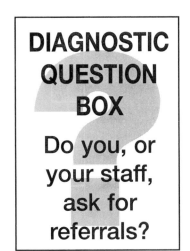

DIAGNOSTIC QUESTION BOX

Do you, or your staff, ask for referrals?

I would recommend adjusting this and giving an attractive discount once the referral has become an active customer. Another modification would be to give the original customer a discount or gift and also give the new customer a gift. This does two things: it thanks and encourages the new customer and, at the same time, gives the original customer confidence in referring your business.

When you send a mailing to a complete stranger, you can only begin it with 'Dear Reader', 'Dear Friend' (cold leads) or some equally impersonal salutation. Please never even think of 'Dear Sir or Madam' which is so impersonal as to be almost insulting. Almost as bad, are salutations like, 'Dear Buyer' or, 'Dear Managing Director'. If you are investing the time in creating a sales letter, invest a little more in a phone call to check the name of the job holder. Most switchboard receptionists will give you this information. You should not depend on printed trade directories for this, as many may be out of date by the time you read them. Online directories should be more current but, even so, look for a 'last updated' note.

When you can write to 'Dear Jill Jones' (warmer leads), you will stand a better chance of the recipient reading the rest of your message.

Unless you are specifically targeting the teen market, keep to 'Dear' rather than 'Hi' or similar informal openers. Even in this market, the parameters of acceptable informality are constantly shifting, so the traditional 'Dear' remains the safest option.

Now, although 'warm' and 'cold' are useful categories for classifying leads, they are too crude to allow you to make truly effective use of your selling time. In a moment we will consider another four subdivisions. But first, we need to consider time and procedures.

Have your procedures in place

You invested time, effort and money in your publicity materials and interest-attracting procedures. Every truly successful business, regardless of size, devotes a substantial amount of energy to creating back office procedures to ensure that:

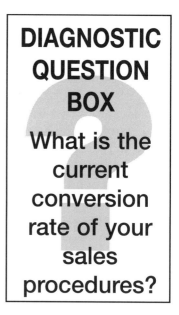

DIAGNOSTIC QUESTION BOX

What is the current conversion rate of your sales procedures?

• All leads are qualified and quantified
• No leads are lost
• Leads are followed up fast

This will only happen when carefully planned and written procedures are in place. This crucial step need not be as daunting as you might imagine. For a sole trader or service professional, these back office procedures may even start as a simple box file or Rolodex of post-cards, or one of the many proprietary computer programs designed to keep track of contacts.

As the business grows, you will need a more sophisticated tracking system. Note that sophisticated does not mean complicated. Your ideal system must be simple, intuitive to use and comprehensive. It must be written down so that you can refer to it when a reminder is needed, and as a guide or monitor to any evolutionary changes that you make, so that it more accurately reflects your needs.

Although you may choose to group your leads together – for example, by geography, source, advertisement or date – your first step is to create one durable paper or electronic record for each lead so that you can track each event from original enquiry right through to the latest sale.

Your procedure must be used to qualify every lead by whichever category is appropriate: by gender, location, date, socio-economic grouping and even customer age, if your product or service is targeted at a particular generation. The word is demographics! These are simply indicators that give you an accurate picture of your potential customers so that you can adjust your future marketing efforts accordingly for better results.

Your sales conversion rate will increase in direct proportion to the amount of information that you know about your prospects.

I suggest you consider this four step categorisation process for your leads:

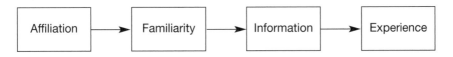

Starting with 'affiliation', move to 'familiarity', then 'information' and finally 'experience', as smoothly and effectively as possible. Let's consider each group in more detail.

Affiliation

These are leads where you do not know too much about the prospects yet, but you already have something in common with them. They may know someone you know, they may share the same leisure interests or they may be members of an organisation to which you belong. You may like to think of them as 'lukewarm' leads as they are already a few degrees above 'cold'.

Familiarity

You are familiar with these leads because you have dealt with them before, either socially or in a business-to-business transaction. You may even have been their client in the past. A useful definition of having reached familiarity is when you know the prospect well enough to know if he or she is married and whether or not they have children. Although this step from affiliation cannot, and should not, be forced, you can still work away at it gently without turning your sales calls or visits into purely social gossips.

Information

Your prospect now knows you well enough to seek information about any product or service that might meet their needs. They will trust you enough not to expect any hard sell, and they respect your opinions if you recommend any third party to them for products or services that you cannot supply yourself.

DIAGNOSTIC QUESTION BOX

How do YOU ensure your company follows up on all your leads?

Always be free with such information. This is something that many consultants are wary of lest the prospect pumps them for free answers instead of booking an assignment! However, when the information stage is reached *after* the two earlier stages, there is enough mutual respect to negate such risks.

Experience

Your prospect has first-hand experience as a result of having done business with you before or second-hand experience because someone they trust has recommended you. When such prospects come to you, you can expect a very high sales to enquiry ratio!

After four levels of customer categorisation, we come to a fifth area which is an absolute no-go area! I refer to 'lost' leads, where someone has contacted you and, for all you know, may be ready, willing and able to place an order. They never get the chance because you simply failed to follow up on their lead and neglected to call them back.

A marketing firm in the US did a test by asking for 'more details please' from 1000 companies advertising in their local trade directory. Less than half even bothered to reply and, of these, only one in ten followed up after providing the initial information – which can be good news for you! If you always follow up your leads, and the prospect has called several other firms, you now only need to compete against fifty per cent of them!

It is time to consider the actual sales process – what happens when you have your prospect sitting opposite you or on the other end of the telephone. We will deal with the negatives first. Here are the commonest mistakes that all sales people have made at some stage in their careers:

- Attempting to sell the wrong product or service for the prospect's needs – avoid this by asking leading questions at an early stage. If you do not have anything that fits the bill, say so!

- Attempting to sell to the wrong individual. You must only sell to the decision maker, key stakeholder or budget holder.

- Disparaging your competition. This is bad manners and you could end up in court

- Cutting prices to get the order. If price is clearly the only issue, discuss ways that you can offer a lower cost alternative rather than immediately going on the discount trail. Once a prospect knows that you will discount, they hold a winning hand and will use it.

- Not recognising the 'ready to buy' signal and talking right through the 'close'. As soon as a prospect is ready to buy, shut up and reach for the order pad or contract.

- Forgetting to ask for the order. (Yes! Really! It happens!)

Very often the fear of selling is far worse than the actual selling. This is something well known to public speakers and performers who may be almost paralysed by stage fright before they make their entrance, but once on stage they shine with enthusiasm and enjoyment which fuel their great performances.

Selling may well be an art, but it is an art that can be analysed and turned into a planned sequence of six stages that must be followed in order. Before I list them for you, here is a tip that most of the successful sales people I know have employed. They acquire and use a basic knowledge of Neuro-Linguistic Programming (NLP) which allows them to quickly establish and maintain rapport with their prospects. Despite its rather technical-sounding name, NLP is ethical and honest – which, of course, you must be and be known to be.

The selling sequence begins when you have a warm lead.

1. Research your records to determine that the prospect really IS a prospect and not a time-waster. It is not always possible to be 100 per cent certain, except in cases where alarm bells ring in your mind. The ideal qualifications for your prospect are that they are interested, willing to buy and can afford to do so.

2. Discover WHO the prospect is and their place in the hierarchy of the organisation when it comes to decision making. MDs, senior departmental managers, buyers and owner-managers are the levels you should aim for. It can take four times longer to sell to a junior member of staff who has to report back to someone higher, because they will never be able to promote your products or services as well as you can. If you operate within the

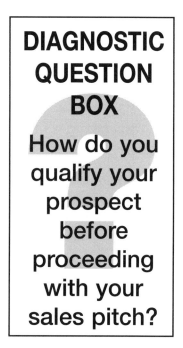

DIAGNOSTIC QUESTION BOX

How do you qualify your prospect before proceeding with your sales pitch?

non-corporate market where your prospect is the ultimate owner and user of what you have on offer, you can skip this step unless there is a partner or spouse involved in the buying decision. Here you should endeavour to make your presentation to both people at the same time.

3. This stage considers the WHAT, WHERE, WHEN, WHY and HOW of matching your products and services to the prospect's needs. Consider how you can deliver on each in turn because the more of the boxes that you can tick in their list of needs, the closer you will come to making the sale. Remember that if you have not asked open questions and been genuinely interested in your prospect you will find this stage a guessing game.

4. Now you present your ideal solution (the best product you have, even if it is the cheapest) and answer any questions fully and truthfully. Then sit quietly and wait.

5. If necessary, offer some alternative solutions if there is still a resistance to making a decision. Avoid offering too many alternatives too soon or you could add confusion and lose the sale. Two options are alternatives. Three or more are choices. Your prospect will find it easier to select from alternatives.

6. CLOSE the sale by asking for the order.

Most of your prospects' objections to your initial sales pitch do not mean 'no'. They usually mean, "yes, maybe, but first I need more information." Your task is to supply it! Guide them to asking specific questions that you must answer equally specifically. Gradually work through their questions until they have no more.

It is more difficult to deal with non-specific objections. "I'll think about it and get back to you" is a common way of a prospect saying 'no' without upsetting you. You have two proven options here. You can ask, "What information do you need to enable you to make your decision to buy now?" or if they are adamant, ask, "If now is not a good time for you, can we fix a time and date and I will get back to you." These both put you back in control of the situation. It can be tempting to throw in a special offer that is only available for a limited period. My advice is to avoid this temptation because it hints of sharp practice and can even suggest that your prices or fees are too high in the first place.

You may be told, "We are considering other suppliers too." Your best antidote to this is to have done your own homework diligently so that you know who your main competitors are – even to the extent of regularly visiting their websites or getting your name on their mailing lists. See if you can elicit the names of the others being considered so that you can then gain an idea of your chances. In a competitive quote or tendering process, the main reasons for choosing another supplier include price, features, benefits and the old-boy network. You cannot do much about the latter, but you can ensure that you match the others before your next presentation. If you do not make a sale this time – and nobody has a 100 per cent success rate – do make sure that you leave something tangible behind to jog their memory and to help keep your name in mind. This could be a brochure, catalogue, reprint of an article in a trade magazine and always, without fail, a business card should be left at every visit.

As an aside, prospects are far more likely to believe something they read as editorial in a magazine, so when your PR (see Chapter 7) results in a good write-up, buy as many copies as you need and send one to all of the former prospects on your list, as well as current clients, with a short note along the lines of, "I thought you would like to see this." You could do the same with other articles that are appropriate to their trade, industry or business. The name of the game is to keep your business in the forefront of their minds.

If price is a key objection, consider offering a lower cost option with fewer features. Note that this is not the same as a discount! Think of the motor industry where most cars are offered in basic, de-luxe and top-of-the-range styles with prices to match.

Note the objections that you encounter and, back at base, consider how you can deal with each of them if and when they surface again. Start with the most frequently expressed objection and work down your list.

If you sense that money is no object, then by all means start with your highest priced option, even if your prospect initially set their target lower. Benefits sell best and features are secondary. In one-to-one personal sales, never make the common mistake of prejudging your prospect's ability to pay. Some of the wealthiest people can also be the scruffiest.

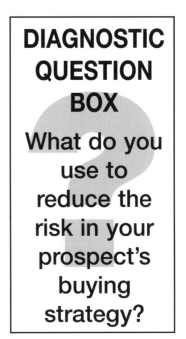

DIAGNOSTIC QUESTION BOX

What do you use to reduce the risk in your prospect's buying strategy?

Every individual who makes a buying decision is also taking a risk. The greater the cost, the higher the risk and, in some organisations, making the wrong buying decision could even cost someone their job or limit their promotion chances. Part of the successful sales procedure is to minimise their risk. The usual way is to offer some sort of guarantee or, at the very least, an element of after-sales support included in the price. If you are offering a personal service, you can offer a 'money back if not satisfied' assurance. It has been suggested that personal sales, especially by mail order, which offer such a guarantee, will outperform those without a guarantee by a factor of two to one. As most people are inherently honest, you will experience very few fraudulent requests for refunds. If you do get a request, pay up promptly and cheerfully to retain your client's goodwill and to enhance your own reputation.

Here are a couple of golden rules for you:

1. **All selling exists to meet a stated and perceived need.**
2. **Always make it as easy as possible for your prospect to buy from you.**

These are so important that you should read them again and learn them by heart.

You need to protect your legal interests and keep your ordering documentation and procedures as simple as possible. Keep all 'small print conditions' to an absolute minimum.

Be patient if your customer's organisation has convoluted ordering systems, as it is worth jumping through their hoops to secure the order. Check to see if you need an official order number and form supplied by them. In many large organisations the orders and payments are processed from a central office. If you can, discover where this is located and get a contact name. This will make it easier if you need to follow up or chase payments.

In the personal or one-to-one marketplace it can be tempting to skip all the paperwork and agree the deal on a handshake. The guideline here is that you can probably do this for low value sales, but for more expensive items and especially where on-going payments are involved, you will do well to have a simple contract document in place.

Here is some insider information that applies to many very large organisations and public sector clients. They tend to have very rigid procedures and annual budgets which typically run from January or April each year. If you can, you will find it useful to determine when their budget year begins.

You may well find that they are flush with funds in the first two months of their budget year. At six months they will produce some half-yearly projections and could find that they need to cut back to stay on target. During the tenth and eleventh months they will experience the 'use it or lose it' syndrome where they are desperate to spend any remaining funds! Your solution is clear; you will be more likely to secure an order during the two months at the start and the end of their budget year. Use the other months to keep them aware of what you have on offer.

You must remain patient. In large organisations the wheels of decision grind very fine and very slowly at times. They may delay for months and then expect you to deliver yesterday! They may also take a long time to settle your account, so do not be afraid to have your own terms of business on each invoice, to include 'Payment within thirty days of invoice date please'. Be prepared to chase your invoice after thirty days as it is often this payment chasing which, if not done, causes cash flow problems. I have added to my invoices 'We reserve the right to claim statutory interest at twenty per cent on the date the debt falls overdue in accordance with the Late Payment of Commercial Debts (Interest) Act 1998.' This act gives small businesses a statutory right to claim interest on late payments from other businesses. This covers my costs for having to chase the payments and, at the same time, adds some weight to my chasing telephone calls.

It is sometimes suggested that one-to-one personal sales can take even longer, as it can take up to seven exposures to your sales message before a prospect finally makes the decision to buy from you.

To return briefly to your own back office procedures, establish the good practice of writing up the outcomes of each sales visit or telephone conversation as soon as possible after the event, regardless of the result. Always, without fail, do this on the same day as the presentation. You never know when you may be invited back and you will find these notes invaluable. If you made a sale, your notes will help you to deliver on what you promised. If you did not, they will help you figure out why, so that you can modify your approach next time and will help you draft any follow up contact letters.

DIAGNOSTIC QUESTION BOX

When do you write up the details of contact with prospective customers?

Still in your back office, a simple alphabetically-arranged filing system will help you project a professional image. This should be within reach of your telephone so that when you receive an unexpected call from a former lead or client, you will immediately have their details in front of you. If you use a computer system it must be fast and, of course, it must be regularly backed up.

Because there is such a diversity of business out there, it is impossible to offer fail-safe selling procedures that will apply to every circumstance. If you sell through mail order you will have different methods and priorities from someone selling in a shop. If you provide a service, therapy or consultancy where there is no tangible end product, by which I mean something that the client can pick up, look at or carry away, your needs will be different again.

Using the principles outlined in this book will keep you on track, but consider modelling success too. This simply means that you keep aware of what is going on in your trade or industry and look for any lessons you can learn from the most successful operators, which you can then imitate or adapt for your own purposes. You may learn even more from one-time competitors who go under, so that you do not make the same mistakes.

There is no profit until a sale is made and paid for!

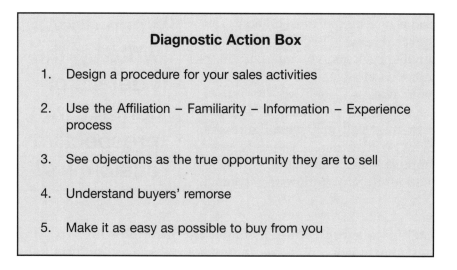

Diagnostic Action Box

1. Design a procedure for your sales activities

2. Use the Affiliation – Familiarity – Information – Experience process

3. See objections as the true opportunity they are to sell

4. Understand buyers' remorse

5. Make it as easy as possible to buy from you

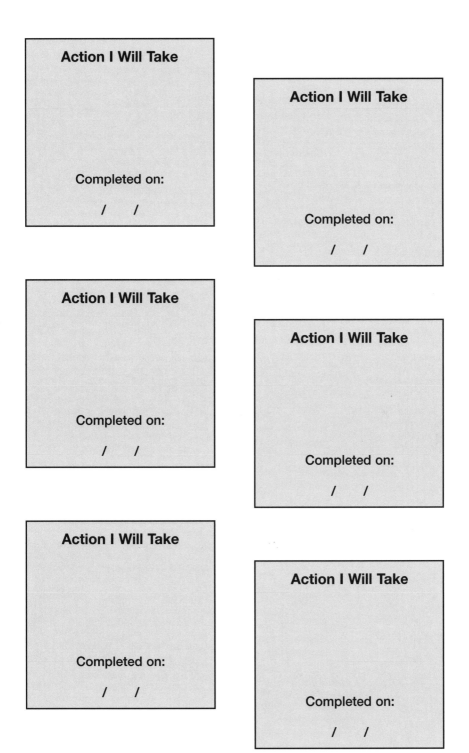

Action I Will Take

Completed on:

/　/

Action I Will Take

Completed on:

/　/

Action I Will Take

Completed on:

/　/

Action I Will Take

Completed on:

/　/

Action I Will Take

Completed on:

/　/

Action I Will Take

Completed on:

/　/

Chapter Six

Marketing Magic

Marketing lays down the first stepping stone that leads to a sale.

Synopsis

This chapter looks at the role of marketing as the first step in customer creation. Marketing is what creates and sustains a demand for your products or services. Sales follow as the result of effective marketing. We examine some of the marketing tools that are available to you, regardless of your business or practice. To set the scene, here is a story about the importance of expectations.

Ann and John White, a young couple, bought a seaside guest house as their first business venture. The estate agent had described it as having 'considerable potential in the right hands'. This meant that it was neglected and run down. The surveyor pointed out remedial work that would be needed in the near future. With innocence and enthusiasm, the couple worked late into the night all through autumn and winter to prepare the premises for their first guests at Easter.

After all the costs associated with their purchase and initial renovations, they could not afford new brochures. Happily, the former owner had left them a box of brochures that he had been using for the last five years.

Our couple followed the former owner's advertising programme too, sending out the simple brochures and accepting bookings. The Guest House opened on time and, after a few teething problems, had a successful summer season with very few complaints.

With a positive bank balance, the Whites commissioned a copywriter and printer to produce new brochures. These were colourful, glossy and contained powerful sales triggers. That winter they placed their new advertisements in more upmarket journals and directories, and the bookings flowed in.

During the second season, although the place was cleaner and the service was better than before, the number of complaints quadrupled. Refunds of deposits were demanded by unhappy guests who arrived, looked and immediately departed.

The couple hired a business coach and together they identified the cause. The original basic brochure had raised expectations to a fairly low level that was commensurate with the fair prices being charged. Guests were delighted to discover that their expectations were exceeded. They enjoyed their stay and left happy.

The revised brochure and luxury market place advertising raised expectations beyond the reality. Arriving guests were dismayed to find that these expectations were not met. Those who stayed tended to look for faults to complain about and, with this attitude, made sure they found some.

John White said, "We learned the hard way. It is important to show the business in a positive light, but it is even more important to under-promise and over-deliver." They reverted to the former brochure style and built a successful enterprise. It became so successful that they were even able to cut back on their advertising spend, as word of mouth recommendations created new and repeat bookings from satisfied guests.

You can have the best premises, products or services in the world. Unless people know that you exist and are open for trade, this is all you will have – no customers or clients, no sales, no profits and very soon, no business. Marketing is what generates an interest and demand; advertising then sustains this interest and reveals how the demand is met.

Within the context of this chapter, marketing means anything you do to stimulate and sustain a demand for your products or services. Advertising is covered in Chapter 8, and means anything you do to make potential clients aware that you are the ideal business to fill that demand. Publicity is what other people might say or write about you, and in the next chapter we look at public relations (PR) which is what you say, write or broadcast about your business.

The Success 'Magic' that You Must Apply to All Your Promotions

The success 'magic' is mentioned in just about every book or seminar on marketing and sales creation. It only appears magic because so many business owners ignore it and then wonder why their promotions do not work.

The magic can be described in just three words: Consistency, Congruency and Testing.

Anything and everything seen by a client before, during and after their contact with your business *must* be consistent. I had one client who used royal blue print on her letterhead, dark green on her website, purple on her business card and orange on her brochures. Then, to compound the error of this rainbow approach, she used several variations of her name, almost at random. (I have changed the name to protect her identity.) She signed cheques as J. A. Blank. She signed letters as Jane Blank. Her business card invited people to call her Jane A. Blank, but in the brochure it said 'Jane Ann Blank is the founding director of JAB consultants'. Her e-mail address was JaneyB!

Anything that creates confusion in the mind of your typical customer/client will delay or destroy their decision to buy from you. They may well go instead to your competitor who uses consistency. This next consistency step can create an amazing increase in your sales and income, and you should take it now while the concept is still in your mind.

- Examine all the variations of your name. Choose ONE and use it for EVERYTHING
- Examine all the variations of your business name. Choose ONE and use it for EVERYTHING
- Examine all the colours that you use. Choose ONE and use it for EVERYTHING

- Examine all the variations of your logo. Choose ONE and use it for EVERYTHING
- Examine all the variations of your font or typeface. Choose ONE and use it for EVERYTHING
- Examine all the variations of your e-mail or web address. Choose ONE and use it for EVERYTHING
- Examine all the variations of your postal address. Choose ONE and use it for EVERYTHING

Here are a few more proven simple and practical tips that can help you with marketing.

- Keep it simple
- Keep it easy for your clients to remember
- Make it easy for your clients to read and respond
- Check that your chosen colour looks good when it is reproduced in black and white, as people will photocopy or fax your materials. If, for example, your company name is always in red against a black rectangle, it will reproduce as just a black rectangle because most monochrome reprographic systems render red as black
- Thin typeface is harder to read than heavier styles. Print this trendy style in white against a pastel-coloured background and, although you might win a few design awards, you will lose countless sales
- The perfect business name states what your business does

Consider this address:

> The G M Company Ltd
> Gidget House
> Perimeter Road
> Anytown Industrial Estate
> Anytown
> Nr Sometown
> Homeshire AB4 5CD

You or someone in your organisation is really going to enjoy finding and typing this when you need a Gidget!

Now consider this:

> Gidget Ltd
> Perimeter Road
> Anytown
> AB4 5CD

Which would you prefer to type?

Before we leave the topic of names and addresses, it is vital that you include your name and address on any marketing materials, even if you run a totally website-based business. You have probably seen a leaflet or flier advertising a home service for, say, drives and patios. It invites you to contact 'Dave' on a mobile phone number. How much confidence will you have? If 'Dave' had included his surname, contact address and landline number you would be 100 times more likely to add him to your shortlisted candidates to do the work.

Congruency is as important as consistency. If you run a small business, do not pretend to be a major organisation because your typical customer/client has different expectations based on perceived size. If you run a '£1 for Everything' store, you will send the wrong message if you use glossy, full colour brochures. In congruency, you will use cheap and cheerful fliers in one colour which will probably be red and read.

Conversely, if you are in the travel business, specialising in luxury holidays, your typical customer/client will expect a prestigious brochure with a luxury feel. Rich, dark shades generally create images of quality. Bright basic colours raise expectations of low cost. Cheap, thin paper suggests bargain basement. Heavy, glossy paper means quality and expense.

Despite the current trends towards political correctness, your promotional material must be congruent with traditional expectations. If you manufacture clothes for baby boys, your typical customer will expect to see light blue as a featured colour. If you sell novelties for little girls, then pink will meet expectations. Any product or service aimed at women will hit the target with shades of pink, lavender or purple. For men, shades of black, brown and grey are favoured. If you buck the trends of these expectations you could raise doubts and lose sales as a result. The exception to this is if you are deliberately setting a trend.

Clearly, you must show your business in the most favourable light, but beware getting carried away into the realms of daydream believing. Congruency means projecting your case well without going over the top.

Let consistency and congruency flow over, around and through your business and allow them to permeate all your business thinking.

> **DIAGNOSTIC QUESTION BOX**
>
> **Do the colours on your marketing match your typical customer expectations?**

Testing is vital. If you plant tomatoes and expect potatoes to grow, you are on a fast track to frustration. Also, if you do what you have always done, you will get what you always got. If what you are getting from your current promotions is not what you want, you must change something.

The key is to change one thing at a time. If you make several changes, you will not know which one did the trick. If your marketing letter is producing many enquiries but few actual orders, try changing the headline. If that does not work, revert to the original headline but change the opening paragraph. Repeat this process until you hit your jackpot.

> **DIAGNOSTIC QUESTION BOX**
>
> **When did you last test the results of your marketing promotions?**

To test your results you must clearly have some means of identifying which version worked for you. Make sure you have a good and clear recording system in place at the start of a campaign. Successful marketers and advertisers know the truth of 'test, test and test again'.

Before we get into the general areas of marketing, I need to clarify a few niche methods that you will come across.

Network marketing

Also known as multi-level-marketing (MLM), this is where a promoter recruits people to sell a product on his or her behalf and at the individual's risk. Each person is then expected to create a chain of others who, in turn, create their own chains. These chains are usually referred to as 'down-lines'. If you are at the top of the pile you get a percentage of the profits earned by everyone below you, just as they get a percentage from those below them.

There are some excellent MLM organisations but, alas, they are vastly outnumbered by others that are designed to appeal to people seeking a 'get-rich-quick' solution. If you are serious about your own business, then this is not the route to go. The exception to this rule is if you have a product or service that has sufficient profit margins to allow many mouths to take a bite – and if you are prepared for the challenges of non-stop recruitment, which you will need to do because of your position at the top of the company.

Affiliate marketing

This is a similar scheme which is usually adopted by internet-based business entrepreneurs. Proceed with extreme caution. The glowing statistics and earning potentials may have been achieved by one or two high-flyers but the average earnings are rarely revealed.

Direct marketing

As the name implies, this branch of marketing means that you contact your typical customer/client directly by letter, e-mail or telephone to elicit an order. Many successful businesses have been built on telephone marketing, but this is a double-edged sword. You may annoy as many people as you attract. Once annoyed, they are unlikely to buy from you.

DIAGNOSTIC QUESTION BOX

How many follow-up letters or phone calls do you do before you quit?

An effective form of direct marketing is this four step process:

1. Invite your typical customer/client to apply for an information pack with no obligation. Include a 'free report' or another special offer to encourage them to respond.

2. Send them the information they have requested and include an order form with the various options for payment. Include a discount for prompt response.

3. If no order arrives within the first three weeks, write again 'in case you mislaid ...'

4. At monthly intervals, repeat step 3 with a different letter. With your final mailing, include a strong 'absolute last chance' message.

Jay Conrad Levinson is one of the most successful marketers in the US, his research suggests your marketing needs to penetrate a person's mind nine times to move them from 'total apathy' to 'eager to buy'.

Now the plot thickens. According to Jay, one out every three messages will not get through. So the first three exposures to your message will score one hit, but your potential customer will do nothing with it. With the following three messages you will penetrate again. Now they realise they have heard of you before, but still do not buy.

I will skip the detailed sums, but here is what probably happens with each batch of three subsequent exposures:

"These people must be successful; they're spending lots on marketing."

"I wonder what else I can discover about them."

"Maybe I should consider a purchase."

"I really should find the money."

"Here's my order."

To penetrate a person's mind nine times, you have to contact them 27 times to convert them from 'apathy' to 'buy'.

The reason that so many entrepreneurs fail with direct marketing is that they quit too soon. Now, personally, I think that 27 contacts is getting dangerously close to pestering, with all the negative connotations this implies. The critical factor is the frequency of those contacts. Weekly intervals will certainly be perceived as pestering or desperation. You may avoid these labels with monthly messages that are delivered as a newsletter that offers news and entertainment, with the plug for your services included almost as an apparent afterthought. As long as your newsletter is not just a serial advertisement or pages from a brochure, recipients will look forward to receiving it.

The message is clear. Direct marketing is not an event. It is a process.

General marketing

This is where you get your message out into the world and attract a few typical customers from the entire population.

General marketing can include:

- Canvassing
- Fliers
- Broadcasters
- Exhibition stands
- Branded gifts
- Circulars
- Directories
- Posters
- Seminars
- T-shirts
- ... and many more. Consider all possibilities as you mix and match to select the method that is best for your business.

Personal recommendation

This is the most powerful, effective and cost-effective marketing method in your toolkit. It is powerful and effective because the person recommending your services will have far more credibility with their network of friends and colleagues than you can ever achieve as a stranger. It is cost-effective because it costs you little or nothing in relation to other forms of marketing.

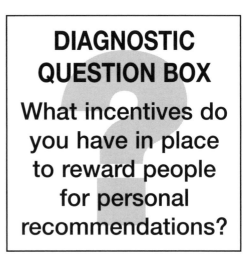

DIAGNOSTIC QUESTION BOX

What incentives do you have in place to reward people for personal recommendations?

To get these valuable referrals all you need to do is ask. Ask at the point of delivery and again when your typical customer/client tells you what a wonderful product or service you have. Consider this: if you ask for one name and contact details, you may get none and you could put your typical customer/client in an uncomfortable situation. Ask for five and they will probably be delighted to come up with two. Always get permission to use their name when you contact their referred person. An alternative is to get a commitment from them to contact the person first to prepare the prospect before your call.

Another very effective way of getting personal recommendations is to give an incentive to encourage the supply of referrals. For example, offer your products in a specially selected referral box containing a referral voucher for your products, a voucher from one of your strategic partners in the high street or simply offer a cash incentive. All of these methods will inspire and motivate people to refer your products or services, and it is a holistic marketing method. Everyone benefits with an incentive marketing referral system.

Much of what you have read here is also applicable to advertising but, given the costly pitfalls that can await an unwary advertiser, this is a subject that demands a chapter of its own.

Diagnostic Action Box

1. Select the style and colours you will use for all your marketing materials

2. Examine all your marketing ideas for consistency, congruency and testing

3. Select one preferred marketing method and put it into practice this month

4. Set up a referral marketing strategy

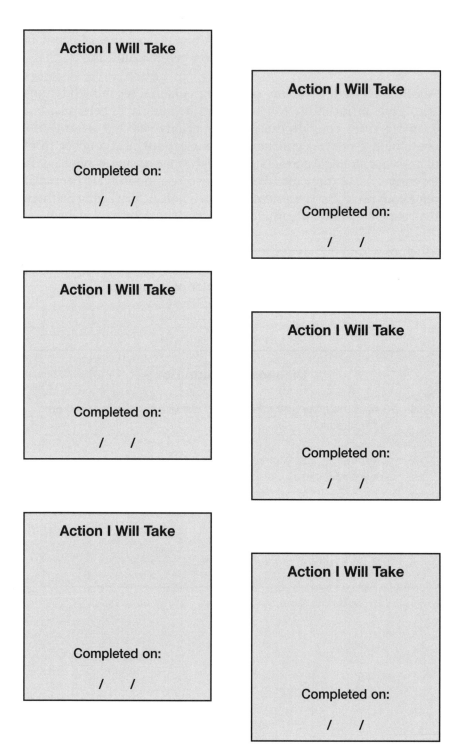

Action I Will Take

Completed on:

/   /

Action I Will Take

Completed on:

/   /

Action I Will Take

Completed on:

/   /

Action I Will Take

Completed on:

/   /

Action I Will Take

Completed on:

/   /

Action I Will Take

Completed on:

/   /

Chapter Seven

Your Press Releases

Press releases are welcomed by the media as a source of ideas and content. Press releases are the best 'free advertising' of all.

Synopsis

This chapter looks at how to understand the principle of press releases and how to use them as a free source of marketing and customer creation. Local newspapers are constantly looking for material and are interested in the smallest changes that you make to your business.

The long established seaside minicab company was struggling. It once enjoyed a healthy seasonal trade from holidaymakers during the summer season but now, fewer and fewer people came for their annual break because it was just as cheap to go abroad. Those that did come tended to have their own cars anyway, so did not need cabs.

The owner recognised that he could no longer keep his eight cars and drivers gainfully employed unless he took drastic action. So he sought an alternative source of passengers. He used 'resting' drivers to leaflet the two large local housing estates and both the major supermarkets in the area. He was able to keep the cars busy, albeit at reduced fares, by running the elderly and mothers with young children between the shops and their home.

Then the supermarkets did a deal with a local bus company to provide a free hourly bus service. Too many cabs stayed in the garage while the drivers bemoaned the loss of income as they sat in the office watching daytime television.

In late November, the owner decided to revive an idea that had worked in the past, just after the introduction of drink-drive legislation.

He would have his wife repair the old Santa Claus outfits so the drivers could wear them. He recalled how children would stand outside the supermarket saying, "We want to ride in Santa's cab!"

The very first driver to go out to collect a fare was pulled over by an alert policeman. He was told that his outfit was illegal because it was impossible for passengers to see if his face was the same as the photo on the driver's ID lapel badge. The owner's first thought was to lodge a complaint, but then he realised that years earlier, when he had dressed the drivers as Santa, they did not need to be licensed or wear any ID.

So he wrote a press release for the local paper. He headlined it: 'Santa's Close Shave' and took photos of the driver in his costume, both with and without the beard. He made sure that the cab with its branded windscreen banner was clearly visible in both shots. The paper sent a reporter round to interview the drivers and ran the story on its front page.

The next week, the local county paper ran the story under the headline, 'Father Christmas Bewhiskered'. The best-selling national tabloid newspaper picked up on the story – 'Santa Nicked For Not Shaving' – which was also followed up by national TV news.

That Christmas was the busiest in the company's history. The newspaper stories were reproduced and enlarged and posted on the booking office windows. The goodwill factor lasted well into the next summer as people rang for cars and invariably mentioned the story. That year, the company took on two new drivers to cope with the demand.

Getting a press release printed in your local newspaper or trade publication is not as arduous as you might think and submissions are often welcomed by the editor. In common with many other organisations, to remain viable, most magazine and newspaper publishers have slimmed their payroll to a minimum. Although this is not good for the journalists concerned, you can make it work to your advantage.

Editors have to fill a given number of pages in every issue of their publication and will welcome well-presented stories that you can provide. They are also very busy individuals, so you will have a far better chance of publication if you present your story in a way that needs a minimum of alteration.

A common mistake is to simply take your advertisement or brochure, write 'Press Release' across the top of it and hope it will be printed. It won't! Instead, you will probably get a call from the advertising department with a suggestion that you buy advertising space.

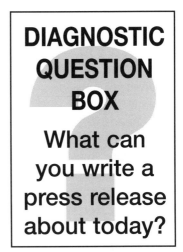

DIAGNOSTIC QUESTION BOX

What can you write a press release about today?

You can increase your chances of publication by always presenting your story as news. Later in this chapter I will share well over twenty tips that will make editors receptive to your words.

If you write your own press releases you can gain valuable free advertising. If you do not feel confident enough to create your own, there are many freelance PR people around who will write them for you. Many of these individuals are ex-editors themselves, so they know what is wanted and how to present it. Their fees are usually modest and a fraction of the cost you would pay for an advertisement.

There are valuable hidden benefits in getting your story published as news. Many people skip advertisements because they think that anyone with a cheque book can have an advert published, as long as it is legal, decent, honest and true. These same people will read 'editorial' and 'news' stories and some of them will be aware that these have earned their places on merit. When your story is published as an editorial, it also carries an implied endorsement by the editor, which adds substantially to your credibility.

Before you even think of writing your press release, consider your target readership – the people you want to contact you for your products or services. What papers and magazines do they read? Even local newspapers tend to have 'departments' of regular features that appear in each issue. A local garage, for example, might send a press release for the motoring pages about its new electronic tune-up equipment. A new pre-school nursery would earn a place in the 'Women's Pages'.

You need to update your initial research into your target publications from time to time. Acquire copies of each of your chosen publications and consider which department your story will fit into best. See if the editor of that department is given a by-line. If not, phone the paper or magazine and ask for the name of their features editor, news editor or whatever. Then always address that person by name.

DIAGNOSTIC QUESTION BOX

What papers and magazines does your typical customer read?

While you are reading through the publications, see if you can detect their particular editorial style and make a note of the typical length of stories that may be similar to your press release. There is little point in writing your release in the style of *The Times* if your local paper has a style more like *The Sun*! There is no point in writing a 1000-word release if most of their stories are 500 words or less.

Now you have done the research and made notes, it is time to consider your press release.

Make time to contact the selected editors and find out how they want you to present the information. Some always insist on written copy, sent in by fax or post. Others want their stories sent by e-mail so that they do not have to type them out again. Some will ask for both methods. Despite the rapid advances of information technology, a written document addressed to a named individual will usually be opened and read. Quite a few publishers still have a single fax or dedicated e-mail computer that is shared by several staff. This means that your story may not even reach the person for whom it is intended.

Go for the broadest appeal by thinking of a topic that will affect or interest most of the readership. What does your news really mean to the local community or the readership? If a member of your staff is retiring after twenty-five years' loyal service, then ask them to look ahead to forecast how the business might change in the next twenty-five years. A story that 'Bob Bloggs Receives Long Service Award' is not really of community interest to anyone except those who knew the man. 'Veteran Trader Sees Bright Future for Anytown' will attract readers.

DIAGNOSTIC QUESTION BOX

Who is the editor of your local newspaper or your trade magazine?

Your headline must first attract the editor. It is the most important part of your press release. The editor may change it for publication to appeal to the broadest possible readership, but that does not matter. Unless you grab the editor's attention within five seconds, your story will not be used. Your headline is what does this and is your key to success.

It is much better to produce a swift 100 words every week, rather than 1000 words each month or quarter for local newspapers. This will also keep reminding the editor that you exist and to call on you for a special feature or an article as their local specialist.

If you find the idea of writing a press release a bit daunting, just think of it as a letter or a report. This will make it easier to write. To get a handle on the story, imagine you are telling a friend all about this great news. Then write very simply, the same way you would talk.

Get maximum mileage from the story. First send it to your local newspaper, then to your regional newspaper. At that stage, if it is of national interest, a national newspaper will probably have picked up on it. If not, send it to national newspapers and magazines. The nationals often glean stories from the local press. The local press rarely run stories that have had their first outing in the nationals. Do not forget that local radio and television stations also need stories to fill their programmes. To get the names of their producers or commissioning editors, just give the studios a call.

There is no problem with sending your press release to more than one publication or broadcaster at a time. The more editors that are exposed to it, the better your chances of publication. Remember to aim to also have your story in your trade or professional magazines and journals.

Get to know the journalists or editors. Ask about their deadlines and publication dates. Simply give them a call and arrange a meeting to discuss their needs. Once they have met you, they will be more disposed to look favourably on your submission. Be professional. There is no point in asking for deadlines and then missing them. And always, without fail, send your story in perfect condition with no grammatical, typing or spelling errors. No editor likes to receive material that has obviously done the rounds before being submitted for publication.

Always assume that what you are doing will be of interest to the publication. Local papers and trade magazines are interested in new employees, new premises, mergers and acquisitions, new promotions, new products, charity fund-raising, and anything else that will impact on your community, profession or both.

Some people imagine their local paper will not be interested in a simple move of business premises. You can make the story interesting by adding the background to the relocation. Perhaps you have moved to a new office block which used to be on an old mill site. You could add in details of the old mill, millers, the dates the mill was active and any interesting things about it, as well as information about your company.

New employees offer press release opportunities too. Perhaps one of your employees had an ancestor who was involved with the mill. Think outside the immediate story to points of interest for the readership. 'New Vet Joins Practice' is not very newsworthy. 'Canadian Vet Chooses to Settle in Anytown' immediately grabs the reader who will read on to find out who and why. When running stories about people, you must always get their written permission first.

Consider what are you doing today, tomorrow or even next month that perhaps you were not doing yesterday. How could you build this into a story to interest local people?

DIAGNOSTIC QUESTION BOX
What is happening in your company this month that you could write about?

Share your knowledge and expertise with the readership. A business coach, for example, could write about some new legislation that will affect many of the readers. An accountant might advise on new inheritance tax law and its effects on homeowners in specific income brackets or in specific locations where house prices fall within the catchments. A builders merchant may possibly share knowledge on new health and safety legislation or new products which could be used in the home. Think about your specialist knowledge. Just because *you* know something really well, do not assume that others in the same business already know it. The general public may not know this information either and may not have seen other implications or connections which you spot because of your experience.

When you write your story, design it along the lines of an inverted triangle, remembering that editors usually cut stories for length from the bottom up. This means that you should not put important details in the final paragraphs.

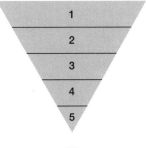

The top part of the triangle (1) is the headline and introduction paragraph. Like all the others, it should end with a 'hook line' to keep the readers' attention and lead them into the next paragraph.

The ultimate 'hook' is your brief, eye-catching headline. If you send your press release as an e-mail, make sure this headline is in the subject box. Editors get loads of e-mails where the sender has written 'Press Release' in the subject box. Do this, and the editor will not be able to find your story easily. Editors often need to find articles in a hurry and if yours is in amongst all the others, you could lose a valuable slot in the publication. Your e-mail subject box should always have your company name followed by a comma and the short headline, like this: 'Achievement Specialists Limited, Business Coach Drives Councillors.'

The first twenty-five words of your press release are known in the journalistic world as the 'introduction'. This paragraph should contain the entire gist of the story, without giving it all away. The objective of this paragraph is to interest the reader enough to read the rest of the article.

Your second paragraph should contain all the stuff you could not fit into the first one. It still needs to keep the reader interested because the third paragraph may be the most important as regards generation of customers.

Your third paragraph is the 'mechanics' paragraph, where the story is really nailed down. The nitty-gritty details like the dates, times and places should appear here, along with your company name and contact information.

The fourth paragraph should be fun, with your opinion or the opinion of another. It should make the story 'fly' by using direct quotes. Always

DIAGNOSTIC QUESTION BOX

What are you planning over the next six months that you could write about?

accompany the quotes with a photograph of the person quoted and always put their job title before their name, like this: "Managing Director, Curly Martin, said business coaching succeeds because it delivers quantified and qualified results." Your opinions are valuable too, and this means you can also be the speaker as well as the author of story.

Your contact details must be in the text of the top paragraphs to ensure that readers can contact you. Do not use headed notepaper because editors never extract your details from your stationery; so unless you put your details within the actual text, they will not be printed. Editors and sub-editors are very busy people who are only interested in the story, not in generating clients for you. You are interested in generating company awareness and clients, so make sure that your contact details make it into print.

Editors are more inclined to print a story that contains live quotes. This is not as hard as it seems; all you need to do is interview one of your current clients. Ask for their views on your move to new premises. Get quotes from people involved in the planning department or local shopkeepers who are affected.

Keep your sentences and paragraphs short. Use around twenty-five words per paragraph and use commas very sparingly. Make it easy for your editor and you will be surprised how often they will use your work.

Throughout your text, use the most critical or headlining words at the beginning of paragraphs or sentences. For example: "Madonna arrives at the Achievement Specialists' offices with her bodyguards behind her" is far more dynamic than, "This evening, at the offices of Achievement Specialists, Madonna arrived with her bodyguards." Keep your language simple. Do not use two long words if one short one will do.

Repeat the point of your message in different paragraphs. This will reduce the chances of it being edited out. Always assume the readership knows absolutely nothing about your topic. You need to explain things which may seem to be obvious to you.

A press release with a picture will always stand a better chance of publication than one without. Consider every opportunity as a photo shoot, then you can use the photographs to accompany any number of press releases. It is better to have a vaguely connected picture than none at all; if you can work animals or children into your story, that is better still. The editor will always have an eye on circulation figures. A paper with a photo of children will sell multiple copies to fond parents, grandparents and family friends.

Always submit colour photographs and opt for action scenes rather than portrait shots. If you are introducing new business premises, then picture your staff walking out of (or into) the office with smiles and waving hands.

DIAGNOSTIC QUESTION BOX

What would make a great action shot for your press release photograph?

If you use a digital camera, aim to set it for medium resolution. The standard of photographs downloaded from the internet is generally not good enough. Send the photographs attached to a separate e-mail with the same subject text so they can be easily identified as belonging together. Always add a caption saying who, what, where and when. The caption for a group of people should always name the people in the photograph from left to right.

If you submit prints, never write directly on the back of them because, when they are scanned for reproduction, the writing may show through. Type your caption on a sticky label and then attach it to the back of the print. Avoid using paperclips and staples as they can scratch the photographs and render them useless. Always shoot the photograph in daylight and send in several examples, as this gives the editor the privilege of selecting the best one for the available shape and space on the page. Shoot both vertical and horizonal pictures as this gives maximum flexibility and a greater chance your story will be printed.

If you lack basic photography skills, call a few local photographers and invite them to quote to do the pictures for you. Remember that even if you commission and pay for the photos, the photographer still retains copyright and may restrict their use. Avoid this problem before it arises by telling your photographer how you plan to use the pictures.

At the end of your story, put, 'Notes to the editor' as this is a really good way of giving background data without cluttering the story. Include all your contact details here too, along with an invitation for the editor to call you for more details or a telephone interview.

Remember that press releases are one of the best forms of free advertising. Your local newspaper editor needs local information, so work to form a symbiotic relationship and produce regular press releases.

To end this chapter, a word of warning. Please do not pester your editors by continuously ringing or e-mailing to find out if they are going to use your story. Some will let you know anyway, a few may even send you a copy of the paper with your story in it. But, for most, you will just have to keep buying the publication and looking to see if it is there.

When your press release story is published, get written permission from the publication to use copies of it in your own promotional packs, press packs and brochures. It will add kudos and credibility to you, your business and your products or services.

Diagnostic Action Box

1. Call the editor of your local newspaper and arrange a meeting to find out the editorial requirements

2. Think of alternative trade publications for which you could produce a press release

3. Decide on a date by which you will have written your press release and have sent it to your chosen editors

4. Then do it!

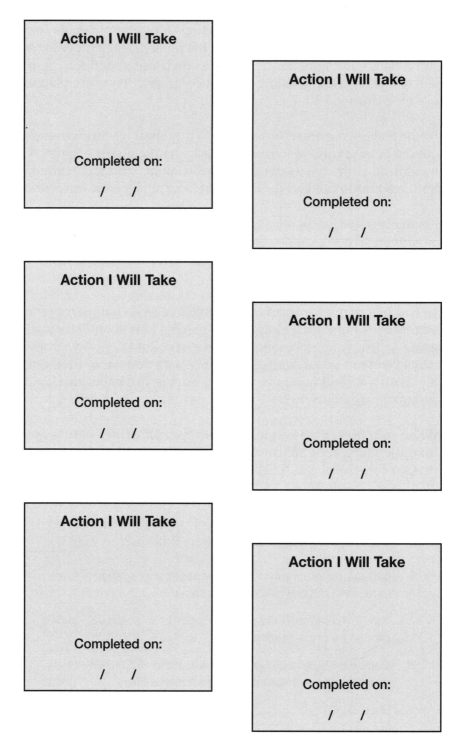

Action I Will Take

Completed on:

/   /

Action I Will Take

Completed on:

/   /

Action I Will Take

Completed on:

/   /

Action I Will Take

Completed on:

/   /

Action I Will Take

Completed on:

/   /

Action I Will Take

Completed on:

/   /

Chapter Eight

The Art of Advertising

Roughly half of all advertising expenditure is wasted.
Here you can discover how to minimise the cost and enhance
the effectiveness of your advertisements.

Synopsis

If you think your business is too small to advertise, it is time to think again. There are several reasons to advertise and countless ways to do it. Read this chapter to discover which method is best for you. As usual, I open this chapter with a true story.

"This is crazy," Mark said. "I can build and install hand crafted and tailor-made kitchens for half the price of the big nationally advertised brands but, every time I visit the DIY warehouse for screws and fixings, I see people queuing up to order their factory made kitchens instead of mine. I cannot afford their advertising budget, so what can I do?"

Veronica, his business coach, quietly stated, "Celebrate your happy difference," then went on to explain that our master carpenter should not attempt to beat the 'big boys' at their own game. With his excellent local reputation and a long track record of high quality work, there was little point in him spending his prime earning time by travelling hundreds of miles, so his first task was to define his local area, a radius of ten miles from his home.

He was to advertise in this area, which would be far cheaper than having a nationwide or countywide campaign. Instead of whole page colour advertisements like the DIY outlets, he would run a small classified advertisement that would be repeated week after week in his local papers. Without knocking the competition directly he would offer to match their written quotations and deliver personal service, backed up by his reputation.

Six months after placing the first advertisement, the sales manager of the local paper contacted him: "You can have a half page adver- torial if you can give me the names of the companies who supply your wood, appliances and electrical installations" (to approach them to sell advertising space).

As Mark's order book filled up for the year ahead, this carpenter was reminded of his favourite saying: 'From little acorns, mighty oaks do grow.'

There are three reasons to advertise. The one that probably first comes to your mind is to attract more customers. The next is to reassure previous customers they have made a good and sound purchase, so that they will recommend you to their friends and return themselves to buy from you again. The third reason is to let everyone know that you are still open for business. That is why it is important to advertise regularly, in the same papers or maga- zines and, whenever possible, in the same part of the publication.

Global conglomerates have a fourth reason, which is to increase market share over their competitors. Constant exposure to their brand names, colours and logos will cause subliminal recognition at the point of purchase, such as the shops or showrooms, and this will create a sale. For the majority of owner-man- aged businesses, we can disregard this fourth reason.

It has been claimed by researchers that most city dwellers in Britain are exposed to around 3000 advertising messages a day. Your advertisement is fighting for recognition, so you need a strategy to ensure you get optimum results.

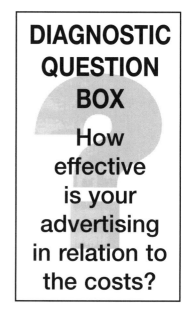

DIAGNOSTIC QUESTION BOX

How effective is your advertising in relation to the costs?

What do you think is the most important part of any advertisement? You obviously need to tell people where they can get whatever you are advertising, but this is not the most important part. If they do not bother to read your advertisement, they will not be interested in knowing where to find you.

You have about three seconds at the most to make a reader stop and read your material. The most important part of your advertisement is your headline. Of course, there will be some potential clients who will be looking for your advertisement because they have already decided that they need or want your products or services. Here your headline is still important – to make sure they spend time reading your message rather than that of your competitors.

Major advertising agencies have a language that is all their own. Even so, you can usefully model a couple of their ideas when you are creating your own advertisements. They speak of your USP, which is shorthand for Unique Selling Proposition or Unique Selling Point. This is simply the offer you have that is unique to your business. In a market place that is crowded with competitors it can be difficult to be truly unique, so think in terms of what you do better, bigger, smaller, brighter, cheaper and more personally than your rivals.

Advertising agencies love demographics. This simply refers to the target reader. Demographics also suggest that everyone can be classified according to disposable income and lifestyles. For example, their top rated 'ABC1' defines affluent, well educated, highly paid, professional owner-occupiers. These probably will not impact on your local advertising, but you may need to familiarise yourself with the term in case it crops up when you are negotiating advertising rates.

Advertising Stages

Writing your advertising copy

Copy is simply a term for the words in your advertisement. The most common error is to write too much. Keep your copy brief and to the point.

Your advertising should have four components. The first is an eye-catching headline. This is followed by the body-copy which simply explains what you are advertising. Here, it is important to focus closely on the benefits of your product or service rather than any technical data. The exception to this rule is when you are selling a technical product, where your readers expect to see some facts and figures. It is a rule that is often broken. Cameras can be technical, but most of their advertisements feature the results you can get, often showing a pretty female model in an alluring pose. Many car advertisements picture the lifestyle that you may aspire to and can allegedly be yours when you buy their latest vehicle.

As an owner-manager, you need not go to such extremes. Just focus on the single biggest benefit of using your business. For instance, if you offer a truly personal service, say so. If you are the only supplier of a product or service in your area, say so.

The third ingredient in a successful advertisement is the call to action. It may be obvious to you, but readers often miss the obvious unless you spell it out. Your call to action simply tells them what to do next – to phone, write or visit, and so on.

Amazingly, the effectiveness of otherwise great advertisements is totally lost by leaving out the essential details of where and how the reader can contact you. The final component you must include is your contact details. If you have a shop and want them to visit, say so. If it is off the beaten track, tell them of a local landmark (next to the police station). If you work from home and do not want them to visit, still give your phone number and e-mail address.

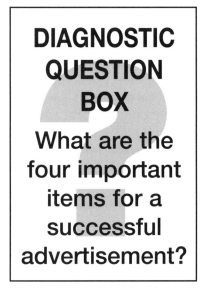

DIAGNOSTIC QUESTION BOX

What are the four important items for a successful advertisement?

Here are some words that have delivered results for advertisers time and time again: *free*, *new*, *exclusive*, *unique*, *improved*, *limited supply* and, essentially, *you*.

For every mention of 'me', 'I', 'my' or 'our', your copy should have at least four instances of 'you' and 'your', because these are the two words that your reader can most associate with. They help to answer their unspoken question: "What's in it for me?"

Before we leave the topic of wording, you should consider the tone and perception of your advertisement. Think of the image that is projected by a lively bar or nightclub that seeks to attract young adults. Compare and contrast this with the tone of an advertisement for a retirement home. Your choice of words must appeal to the readers that you aim to attract.

Should you use pictures? Generally these are best avoided in press advertisements. They add significantly to the cost but add little to the effectiveness. However, you may wish to include your logo or trade mark, which will increase your brand awareness.

Placing your advertising and getting the best deals

Unless you are providing a product or service throughout the land, you can forget about the national press and magazines and focus your attention on local publications. If you do go the 'national route', the following comments about negotiating the best deals will still apply.

All publishers, without exception, have a 'rate card' which sets out their standard advertising prices for various sizes and parts of their publication. It is essential to compare these on a like-for-like basis when you are considering buying space. Alas, this can be a difficult task.

Some rate cards offer readership figures, others mention circulation – both could be exaggerated.

To arrive at a readership figure, the publisher takes the numbers of copies that are printed and assumes that, say, three people read each one. So, a 'readership of 100,000' may conceal that only 33,000 copies are printed. If 33,000 copies are printed, the chances are that up to half of these may be returned as unsold, making the true circulation figure as low as 16,000.

The best publications will tell you their 'ABC Audited Circulation' which will generally be pretty accurate, although, just because they sold thousands of the copy with a cover picture of the current pop star, it does not follow that future circulation will reflect past best performance. The circulation figures matter so that you can calculate your 'cost per reader' and I recommend you assume just one reader for each issue.

As a canny advertiser, you will never pay the prices shown on the rate card anyway. It is sometimes said that everything in life is negotiable. Rate card prices are always negotiable.

Consider the example of your eighth page classified, semi-display advertisement. There is only one place that you really want to be. This is on a right-hand page, in the second half of the publication, in the bottom right-hand corner. By the way, if you are inviting readers to fill in details on a coupon and send it to you, this is the essential place to be.

You telephone the advertising sales department, aware that the boys and girls manning the phones are very highly trained, talented persuaders and, possibly, highly motivated with generous commissions. Your conversation may resemble a tennis game. You serve by asking about advertising. They respond with a high rate card price. You begin to negotiate. They either return your shot with a willingness to consider options or put the ball out of play by insisting on the published price. In this case, you leave your details and move on to the next publication. Within a few days, your original opponent will call you back with a 'final' improved offer.

DIAGNOSTIC QUESTION BOX

What do you look for in the way of discount when placing your advert?

You still have a few tricks up your sleeve. No paper or magazine can publish an issue with blank spaces, so the nearer it gets to their printing date, the cheaper the price of any unsold space becomes. Find out which days of the week or month they go to print and ring them again a couple of days beforehand. A variation on this theme is to negotiate a price for them to keep your advertisement on file so that they can run it whenever another advertiser drops out. Such space will typically cost less than half the normal price.

It is a golden rule of advertising that little and often is better than big and rarely. Use this to your advantage when negotiating prices and seek a significant discount for a series of advertisements that will run in every issue, in the same position, for six months or a year.

A consistent position is always desirable. Let us say that you need a chimney sweep. You recall that you have seen one advertised in your local free paper but, back then, you did not need him. You reach for this week's copy and there he is, in the same paper in more or less the same place. Your readers may not need or want your services the first, second or third time that they see your advert. Even so, their minds will register that they have seen it and they will seek you out when a need arises. They will look in the same spot or on the right-hand pages because they are familiar with your advert being on the right-hand page. So you had better be there!

Getting your press advertisement for free

This is possible, but not through the generosity of the publisher. I know of the owner of a wool and crafts shop who was sharing a coffee with a representative who had called to take an order. In conversation, the representative let slip that his company had a budget for co-operative advertising. They would match half the cost in return for a mention of their particular brand.

The shop owner contacted her other suppliers to see if they had similar arrangements. The result was a free

DIAGNOSTIC QUESTION BOX

What is the publishing deadline for your local newspaper?

half-page advertorial, which was an article about the amazing range the small shop had to offer, surrounded by advertisements from each of the suppliers. The suppliers' contributions paid for the whole feature. This required a double negotiation, first with the publication and then with each supplier, but it was worth it. The resultant free exposure would have cost £2,000 at rate card prices.

Recording your successes

Once you have placed an advertisement or an advertorial, set up a recording or measuring system to track the sales related to the advertisements. The system needs to be recorded at the point of sale. A couple of questions your or your staff could ask include: "How did you hear about us?" or "How did you know about this promotion/product?" and all the answers are recorded. Your staff need to be trained to ask and record the responses to enable tracking and measuring to take place. Once you know the returns on your investment you can decide to continue or change. An advertising campaign without a recording system is like taking photographs with a blindfold over your eyes – you have no idea what is going on.

Beyond the printed page

Press advertising is usually the most affordable media, but consider some alternatives. If you have an appointment in a town that you have never visited before and travel there by train, you will arrive at the station with several needs in mind. You will need a great coffee, maybe entertainment and a meal later, somewhere to stay and a cab to get you there.

Most railway stations have A2 or A3 sized poster sites. If you have a coffee shop, restaurant, cinema, theatre, hotel or taxi service, contact your local station for advertising details. They may even recommend a local printer who will produce your posters for you. There is scope here for strategic advertising alliances. Many taxi drivers are asked to recommend hotels or restaurants. If you are in the catering trade, see if you can negotiate a swap-advertising deal with the taxi company. You put their advertisements in your premises and they put yours in their cars. If you have a major car park near your premises, consider similar small poster advertising or even having your message printed on the pay-and-display parking tickets.

Television advertising costs may be prohibitive for most owner-managed businesses but radio and cinema advertising can be viable propositions. These organisations will have rate cards, but beware the hidden costs. The rate cards will

DIAGNOSTIC QUESTION BOX

What subject do you know about in which you can promote yourself to your local radio as a specialist?

show the price for each number of commercial airings or screenings. They will not always show the production costs of creating your commercial, which can be many times greater.

It is always worth contacting your nearest 'talk radio' station to offer your services as their resident 'expert' on coaching, knitting, cooking or whatever your business has an interest in. There is usually an opportunity to get a sales message across during your interview. There is a New York taxi driver who now has a syndicated five-minute radio slot in every English-speaking country. Known as the 'Gabby Cabbie' he talks of New York life but always includes a plug for his personally guided city tours.

Do not overlook exhibitions and trade shows as a means of advertising your business. To keep costs down, never hire chairs, furniture, stands or electrical equipment from the show organisers. Book 'space only' and take your own gear with you. Book your space as late as you dare because prices fall as opening date approaches. Consider sharing costs and space with a non-competing business colleague. Always put your brochures and sales information in the press room on the first day and keep supplies topped up regularly. Use your best sales staff on your stand and work the room to attract people to your display. If the show has seminar theatres, offer your services as a guest speaker and, of course, tell the audience where to find your stand, which must have a genuine special offer for the duration of the show.

The three main reasons to advertise are to attract more customers, reassure previous customers and let everyone know that you are still open for business. Advertising is a must for business success and growth. This also includes websites and sponsorships such as Google™ adverts.

DIAGNOSTIC QUESTION BOX

What are the total costs of advertising in your local cinema, including production costs?

Whatever the medium, remember the four things your advert must have and enjoy the creativity involved!

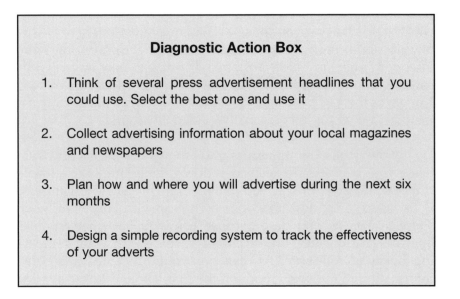

Diagnostic Action Box

1. Think of several press advertisement headlines that you could use. Select the best one and use it

2. Collect advertising information about your local magazines and newspapers

3. Plan how and where you will advertise during the next six months

4. Design a simple recording system to track the effectiveness of your adverts

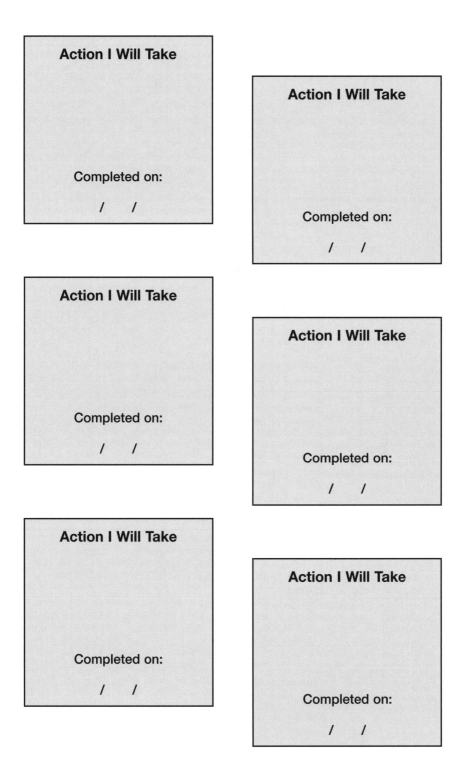

Action I Will Take

Completed on:

/   /

Action I Will Take

Completed on:

/   /

Action I Will Take

Completed on:

/   /

Action I Will Take

Completed on:

/   /

Action I Will Take

Completed on:

/   /

Action I Will Take

Completed on:

/   /

Chapter Nine

Website Marketing

The internet has revolutionised buying and selling by bringing a worldwide market place to your home or desktop. Most businesses, including yours, can benefit from website marketing.

Synopsis

Your website is like a virtual shop window that is open twenty-four hours a day, but it can only work for you if people know that you are there and that you are open for business. Then they must be able to find your site easily. Your job is to ensure that they stay long enough to consider dealing with you, that they return regularly to see your latest offers and that you make it easy for them to place their orders. Then, as with all your transactions, you must process orders and enquiries promptly, courteously and professionally.

Sarah West was sitting quietly in a bar when she noticed two business people who were of similar age and social status, well presented and successful yet not flaunting their wealth.

She overheard their conversation: "Have you taken a look at my website yet?"

"Yes, it looks great, but I wonder how well it is working for you? I spent a fortune on mine and it was a waste of time"

"In the six months since I launched my website, my trade has trebled."

Because Sarah was polite and not given to eavesdropping, she moved on and left the bar. But the snippets of overheard conversation made her think. Why would one website have failed while the other delivered results?

It might be claimed that having any website is better than having none at all. This may well be true unless your site reflects badly on you and your products or services. If you already have a website you may wish to use the signposts in this chapter to see how well it follows them. If you are about to launch one, my aim is to help you begin in the most effective way.

My local bookshop has well over 100 titles on various aspects of website design, development, operation and marketing. Some are so technical that you feel as if you need a degree in computer science just to read the introductions. Others are aimed at global corporations and major organisations and institutions. This chapter cuts through the jargon and takes a basic, common-sense look at website use and abuse.

Here is a question for you. It is simple but the answer may not be easy. Why do you want a website? Here is a clue. The only wrong answer is "because everyone has one these days, don't they?" Beyond this, there is no totally right or wrong answer, only the answer that is right for you at this moment.

There is another clue to be found in the www prefix to all website addresses. It stands for 'world wide web' and is great if you have products, services or even messages to share with the entire world. If you run a small business and deal only with local people you may think that you do not need this international presence. You would be wrong.

> # DIAGNOSTIC QUESTION BOX
> ## Why do you want a website? Is it to sell, inform and entertain, or something else?

As more and more people have access to a computer at work or home, they use the internet in much the same way that they used a printed directory. They need a plumber, a builder, an electrician, a poodle parlour, a coach or whatever, so they use their favourite search engine (more on search engines later) and type in, 'plumbers in Anytown' and within seconds they have several to choose from. If you are a plumber and you are not listed, you may see your business trickling away. The main purpose of having a website is to make information about your business available to potential customers.

Where to start

A key consideration is your website's name or address, which fulfils the same function as your own name and postal address. But whereas you probably had little choice with either of these, you have considerable choice when it comes to your web address. However, as it is unique, you may not always be able to register your first choice. That is when your creative thinking will pay dividends. If you already have a trading name, the best option is to use the same name for your website. Here I should add that I am not obsessed with plumbers, but they do provide an example that almost anyone can relate to.

Stopblock Plumbing Services would thus seek a website address like www.stopblock.com or www.stopblock.co.uk. The advantage of the .co.uk suffix is that potential clients will not waste time looking at plumbers from other countries, which might frustrate them, especially if they are already up to their ankles in water from a burst pipe.

Anyone can use the .com suffix regardless of domicile, but .co.uk is restricted to sites owned in this country. Many television-related businesses register their name with the suffix .tv. This simply means that their site is registered in the rapidly disappearing reef island of Tuvalu which derives most of its overseas income from having this fortunate pair of initials assigned to it.

Although the internet is largely unregulated, there are certain restrictions concerning the use of suffixes to prevent organisations passing themselves off as something they are not, with the intent to deceive. Use .com if you can, or .co.uk or .net. I usually buy the .com and .co.uk and if available .net, because it ensures traffic looking for my company finds it more easily without having to remember the suffix.

To return to the main part of your website name, simple is best. At some stage a potential customer may need to type it on their computer keyboard. Something like 'Xlotledooplebangpooper' will drive them crazy so, in the unlikely event that this is your company name, consider abbreviating it to xdp.co.uk or similar for your website. Having selected, purchased and registered your website name (also known as your domain name) you

DIAGNOSTIC QUESTION BOX

What is your website name?

need to let people know about it. The easiest way is to include your website details on every piece of paper that you send out: letterheads, compliment slips, business cards, brochures, advertisements and even your trade vehicles. People will often remember and use a brief website address, even if they forget a phone number and, of course, they will find the phone number anyway when they visit your site.

The other way to get your name out there is to be listed on a search engine. A search engine is simply a massive computer database of website addresses. As I write, Google™ and Lycos® seem to be the most popular search engines. There are even some, like the oddly named Dogpile®, that will search dozens of other search engines to give you an even bigger variety of sites to choose from.

The aim of most website owners is to get themselves listed at, or near, the top of each search engine listing and, no matter how devious their antics may be, the owners of the search engines are usually one jump ahead. That is why they regularly alter their list sequencing criteria. A further option is to take a paid advertisement on their site but this can be an expensive way of doing things.

You might also consider banners and links. These are where your website is mentioned on somebody else's. As part of their customer service, a ladies' hairdresser might well come to a reciprocal arrangement with a beautician or therapist where each offers a banner or link to the other's site. The downside of this is that a casual seeker of information may leave your own excellent site to visit an interesting sounding link and never come back – especially if you are called 'Xlotledooplebangpooper!'

If we assume that you have a website name and that it is being promoted, what do people find when they visit your site?

The very first thing they find out is how long it takes from them hitting the appropriate keys for something to appear on the screen. Just because you may have a state-of-the-art computer with a high resolution screen and super-sonic broadband connectivity, many of your website visitors may not. In fact, it is best to assume that most of them will not. So throw them a KISS, standing for Keep It Simple Surfers.

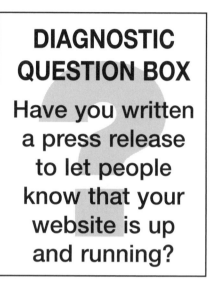

DIAGNOSTIC QUESTION BOX

Have you written a press release to let people know that your website is up and running?

You may want to have a website that wins design awards for its dazzling display of innovative graphics. Your site visitors want information. They want it fast and they want it simple. If yours does not measure up to these criteria, they will simply move on to one that does. The more whistles, bells, special effects, audio clips and video movement that you add to your site, the slower it will load, the less easy it will be for your user and the more it will cost you.

The simplest site of all has just one page. It says who you are, where you are, what you do, why your visitors need it and how to get in touch with you – and it says it all in around 200 words, which is about one screen of easy-to-read type. Depending upon your line of business, you may want a second page, in matching style of course, that makes an offer to encourage the reader to do something like give you their e-mail address (then you can send them future promotional mailings), place an order or request more information. The tip here is that you must clearly tell them what to do, in the same way that every printed advertisement must have a call to action.

The architecture of your site needs buttons for 'next' or 'back' and, if you have more than one page, a menu of options that is permanently on one side of the screen so that your visitors can click on to whichever suits them, without having to read the entire page.

If your site is intended to attract orders, you will need to include some security programs to keep personal data confidential (addresses, telephone numbers, credit card or banking details), an auto-responder that says 'Thanks for your order which has been processed and will be shipped to you in x days,' 'Some data was missing, please re-enter highlighted items,' or 'If your order has not arrived within seven days, click here for latest information.'

DIAGNOSTIC QUESTION BOX

Does your www address appear on all of your printed materials?

Your credit card merchant agreement will contain some essential conditions and many banks will have free information available that specifically concerns internet trading. Listen to the people who specialise in this area. Other alternatives are established companies such as PayPal and WorldPay. Have a surf around, compare charges, terms and conditions and find the most suitable for your business.

Ideally, you want people to return to your site time and time again, so that you are gaining recognition in the name and fame game. Ask them to subscribe to a free report or newsletter that you send them by e-mail. Tell them there is a special offer every month, and then make one.

I was thinking of subscribing to a magazine. Their website said, 'To see our latest issue, click here.' I did, and was presented with a three-year-old copy! Your site must be regularly updated and any seasonal or time-sensitive material removed when its time is up.

Never think that you can take the short cut of simply posting your existing brochure on your site. The psychology of decision making is different for printed, audio or internet text. The choice of words matters a great deal. A brochure is read at leisure and may be seen several times. Your internet message is in a fast medium where you have around seven seconds to grab attention before the next button is clicked and your message is ignored. The best possible advice I can offer is for you to recall that you too

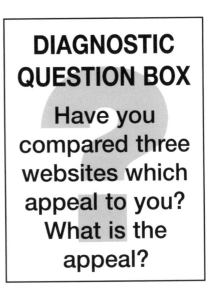

DIAGNOSTIC QUESTION BOX

Have you compared three websites which appeal to you? What is the appeal?

are an internet user. See which sites attract you and ask yourself why. Then borrow the best design features from each of them. But never steal someone else's intellectual property, pictures, drawings or words. It is fine to be similar, but essential to be different.

Your site will need to be hosted. This simply means that it is held on a massive computer bank by your host so that it can be sent in fractions of a second to any computer user that asks to see it.

Costs of this service vary enormously. Some are free as long as you include advertisements for somebody else – but do not even think about it because you will annoy your visitors. Some cost around £1 a month for a very basic site and your budget will control the upper end of the scale.

Many popular computer magazines carry advertisements for website design and hosting packages, and reading these is probably the most painless way of absorbing the jargon and option information. If you prefer to use your computer, enter 'website hosting' in your favourite search engine and see what comes up. Better still, if you have a friend or associate who already has a successful site that attracts new clients, ask them who designed it, who hosts it and how much it costs.

Even in the electronic world of information technology, personal recommendation is still the best advertising of all.

Finally, here are three ways to drive traffic to your website if you are on a budget.

1. Write articles for e-zines, your own weblog, magazines, professional publications, trade magazines, corporate magazines and anywhere you can get exposure for free. An e-zine is an online internet magazine rather than a printed one.
2. Targeted e-zine advertising. Only select the e-zines for your target market and include easy links to your site or the product page you are advertising.
3. Pay-per-click search engines will easily get traffic to your site. Set yourself a tight budget and avoid getting hooked into the bidding game as you will blow a hole in your budget before you know it.

A website is a marketing tool and a shop window – remember to dress your window frequently and with care.

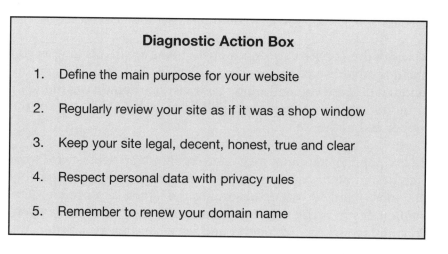

Diagnostic Action Box

1. Define the main purpose for your website

2. Regularly review your site as if it was a shop window

3. Keep your site legal, decent, honest, true and clear

4. Respect personal data with privacy rules

5. Remember to renew your domain name

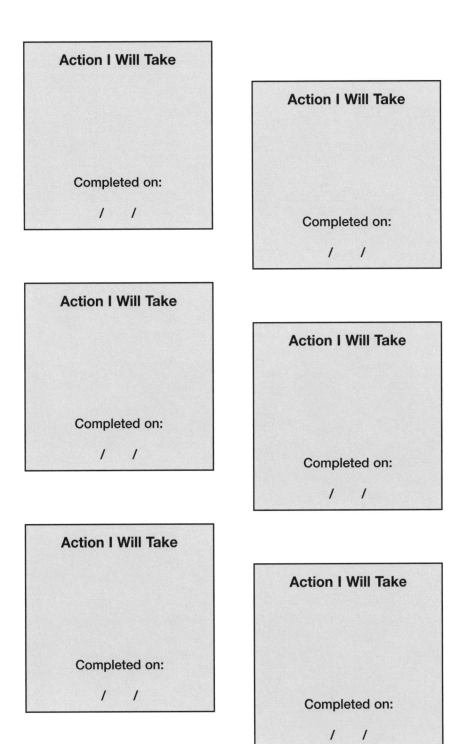

Action I Will Take

Completed on:

/   /

Action I Will Take

Completed on:

/   /

Action I Will Take

Completed on:

/   /

Action I Will Take

Completed on:

/   /

Action I Will Take

Completed on:

/   /

Action I Will Take

Completed on:

/   /

Chapter Ten

Tactical Socialising

*Where networking can be passive and often feels 'hit and miss',
tactical socialising is a focused outcome-oriented activity.*

Synopsis

**This chapter covers an effective method to increase your profile
with tactical strategies and the TACTIC model. Many businesses
rely on a haphazard way of building business contacts and therefore getting contracts. Tactical socialising uses strategies to get
you to the right people.**

Stuart Downing was standing in line at the refreshment table and
started a conversation with the guy behind him.

"Hi, my name is Stuart. How did you find that last session?"

"Oh, hi. My name is Julian Booker. Well, it was a little long but I
enjoyed the bit on springle sprockets. How about you?"

"Well yes," replied Stuart, "I am enjoying it. I have been asked to talk
at the Printers' Annual Conference and I am picking up ideas for
the talk. To be honest with you, I am a little nervous speaking in
front of some of the country's finest."

To Stuart's surprise Julian Booker was one of the committee members organising the Printers' Annual Conference. Julian arranged to
meet Stuart that evening and he gave him some valuable advice and
guidance on how to customise his talk for the audience. Julian also
offered to introduce Stuart to some of the committee members, one
of whom gave him the largest order his company had ever received.

Tactical socialising is based on the belief that you need to build and grow your contact list using the kind of tactics that powerful people use. The effectiveness of your contact list is directly a result of the methods and strategies you use to grow and develop it. I think that many business owners do not consciously work on their lists because they tried it once (joined a networking group) and either did not like it or did not understand the benefits of growing the list and selecting targets from the list to focus on.

Targets are the people who fit your typical customer profile as described in Chapter 4, or people who have access to your typical customer.

People often confuse socialising with networking and then they blend the two. Sometimes they get lucky and other times they do not. Tactical socialising involves knowing what your purpose is, identifying people who can help you achieve it (your target) and focusing on using all types of socialising to win over your target, a sophisticated blend of socialising *and* networking.

The Uncompromising Network

Tried it once and did not like it

My first response to this is 'Get over it!' There are several reasons for not liking the meeting or seminar that you attended. It could be the members were not particularly friendly, they were too demanding, they were from the wrong business sectors, member-ship was too expensive, the meetings were far away and perhaps you did not get any business. The main thing about becoming a member of any group is to attend it a couple of times before actu-ally joining and tactically select a group according to your target market strategies. Also, you may not come away with business from the first, second or third visits because you will need to build trust and friendships, and this can take time. Just go along to enjoy it and spend your time identifying targets to connect with later.

Five reasons for tactical socialising

1. Your targets may be able to help you achieve your outcomes.

2. If you ask politely, your target may display your marketing materials and/or products and by so doing, will be seen to endorse them.

3. If you ask politely, your target may promote your services or products, especially if you offer them a commission on sales.

4. It gives you the opportunity to connect with contacts that could become your sponsor and arrange a meeting for you with your targets.

5. Strategic partnerships often start from disparate meetings.

Tactical strategy 1 – Who's who?

Who do you already know? Go through your address book along with your contact lists and remember to look back at old address books or diaries, old business cards, etc. Make an up-to-date list of your contacts.

Tactical strategy 2 – Purpose

Before you start communicating with the people on your list be sure that you fully understand your purpose. What is your outcome for tactical socialising? Be clear on your products and services and know exactly which market you are targeting. It is always easier to identify and pursue one target market at a time. This keeps you focused, allows you to identify a successful approach and enables you to repeat the process (without having to think too much about it) during this specific market campaign. Know your competition and consistently keep up-to-date with their marketing and sales promotions.

Tactical strategy 3 –Story telling

Identify one or two of your achievements. Look for achievements in your past where you have overcome some embarrassing situation or where you surmounted an uncommon challenge. It is much more effective when telling a story about yourself, to reveal a personal and perhaps private incident. This demonstrates to your audience that you are open, human and that you trust them with this information. As it creates an atmosphere of trust, your audience will be more inclined to give you business. You need to

DIAGNOSTIC QUESTION BOX

What personal story are you willing to share to build rapport?

remember whom you told the story to, so keep details of your contacts and what stories you have told them. You do not want to tell the same story to a group of people where one of the group has already heard it. That will dent your credibility and could reduce your chances of new business. Therefore, you will need more than one story.

Tactical strategy 4 – Matrix model

Take out the list you created in tactical strategy 1 and put the contacts in a matrix (see opposite). I have divided this matrix into three categories (information, social and sales opportunities) and you can select categories to suit your outcomes or purpose.

Information – in this column I would put anyone who could be a source of tactical information. In my own information column list are authors, consultants, trainers, regulators, lawyers and members of institutes/committees/boards.

Social – this column holds all the people I know who would help me and with whom I already socialise: family, friends, people

Name	Information	Social	Sales opportunities
John Smith	Member Institute of Directors	Mentor, Cricket club	Julian Graves at Cricket Club
Sally Black	Member of Chartered Institute of Purchasing and Supply		Supplier
Tim Tanker		Ex colleague (Springles)	
Peter Pool		Church warden	Satisfied client

I have helped, club members, church members, ex-colleagues, mentors, gym members, et al.

Sales opportunities – in this column I list all my satisfied clients, staff members, my suppliers, people I have given business to (non-suppliers, hairdressers, tailors, et al.), people I have referred and any business referral group members.

Remember to keep your matrix up to date and add all new contacts to the matrix immediately after you have met them. Work with a current list and you will remember who is who and who knows whom.

Tactical strategy 5 – TACTIC model

This model is based on getting to know more about the people you know. It will help you to distinguish what is important about, and what is important to, the people on your list. It will enable you to help them to succeed, and will help you to target tactically thus reducing wasted time on mismatched meetings. You need to keep details of your contacts and a record of when you spoke to them last. If you are keeping records you may need to register in line with the Data Protection Act 1998. The TACTIC model gives you guidelines on what you should be keeping records of and therefore the information you need to obtain when speaking to a target.

T Talents and skills your target may have. What are they? Will they help you now or in the future? It is sometimes easier to find out from acquaintances by saying, "I've heard Fred is good at xxx?" and, if that does not give you enough, add "How does Fred do it?"

A Aims and goals of your target. If you know what they want to achieve and can help them achieve their aims, they will in turn help you. For example, you have a CD audio program on time management and your target mentions they are going to tighten up on this area. Lend or give them a copy of the program as a gift. This is a judgment call by you; if giving it as a gift could be seen as *too* friendly, just lend it.

C Challenges that currently face your target – can you help with your knowledge and contacts? Fred mentions he has had a hell of a day. Ask if you can help. He is likely to tell you about the day and you get more information. For example, he has been tasked with opening (getting sales) the wet leisure market in an area where you are a member of the sailing club and you know someone who is connected in a way which might help.

T Tracking the routines of targets is important. If you know your target will be in the golf club on a Wednesday afternoon, you know when to go.

I Interests and hobbies are a great way to meet targets and at the same time learn something new in an enjoyable manner. Interests include any sport, charity work, religious affiliations, films, theatre, music, travel, etc. It is easy to strike up a conversation about interests and often you just need to listen. If the target is very important to you, put the time in and learn, join in or volunteer in your target's hobbies or interests. Be seen at the events and get someone at the event to introduce you. Avoid approaching the target directly. Always get introduced as it makes a better impression. Ask the organiser or anyone you have seen speaking in an amiable manner to the target: "Could you introduce me to Fred please?" If asked why, make sure you have done your research and know his current challenge and have something you can offer to help. "I heard he was interested in xxx and I think I can be of some assistance."

C Connect as soon as you can with your target by asking open questions and actively listening to the reply. If you have to introduce yourself always make a compliment followed by a question. "Hi, my name is xxx. I hope you do not mind my introducing myself as I heard you are a specialist in xxx pause (respond if diverted). How did you get into the field?" Then listen!

Tactical strategy 6 – Who and what is missing

Identify what is missing from your lists that you need to achieve your purpose. You are looking for skills, contacts, memberships, locations and anything that you need to support you. If you have decided to expand into the South having only targeted the North, who and what helped you succeed in the North? Will the same types of people with the same skills and information help you in the South? Who is successful in the South? Find out who can help, decide your strategy and target them.

Tactical strategy 7 – Target tactics

When you know your purpose and goals (Chapter 2) you will become very aware of the areas in your business which need extra input. You will be able to identify who will be best placed to help you. If you already have a good relationship with this target you can simply approach them with your requests and go to work. If, on the other hand, you do not yet have a relationship with this target or the relationship is weak, you will need to develop it to the point where you

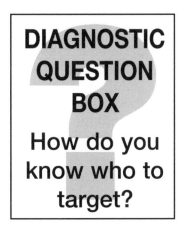

DIAGNOSTIC QUESTION BOX

How do you know who to target?

can broach the subject of the target helping you reach your goals. To do this you will have to do some research on the target to build a profile you can work with. The ways to obtain background information are to ask people who know the target, to read the target's annual accounts, to do an internet search, look and listen. Once you have a profile on what your target does on a professional, personal and public basis you can then plan your approach by selecting appropriate methods of contact.

Seven target tactics – ways of getting to your target and building a relationship

1. Clubbing – join the same clubs as your target. Start by getting yourself introduced or by just simply saying "Hi" when you pass them. Remember you are going for a long-term relationship and therefore you must take your time. Watch very carefully how your target reacts in this environment. Who do they talk to mostly? Where do they spend time? What type of person is your target – extrovert or introvert? You need to adapt your approach according to the way your target normally behaves. Remember, your target will need to feel comfortable, safe and secure before they will engage with you, and it is your responsibility to create this atmosphere.

2. Enlisting – you can enlist your target, based on their background and experience, for a non-executive board position or as an advisory board member. If they are a known speaker you could ask them if they would like to speak at one of your events, or just invite them to the event and enlist their help to pick out the winner of the charity draw (the charity should be your target's favourite charity).

3. Seeking counsel – asking your target for advice or opinion. Everyone loves to feel respected and admired and you can show this by simply asking your target for their valued opinion or advice on a topic. The subject should not be an area for which your target would normally charge for the information. This is very important. You are not there for a freebie, you are there to build your relationship.

4. Requeting information – this can be used in two ways. You can use it to get your target to work with you and you can use it to find a resource. If your target supports a children's charity, for example, and you have the free use of a bouncy castle for a day, use this opportunity to ask an indirect question which will help you to build rapport without seeming gushy. Ask: "Do you know anyone who can make use of a free bouncy castle for a day, as I have access to one and would like it to go to a good cause?" By asking any of the following questions you will give your target the opportunity to either put themselves

forward or give you a name of another prospective target. Questions which start with "Who do you know...?", "Who do you know who lives near...?", "Who do you know who has the skill...?", "Who do you know who has experience of...?", usually give you a satisfactory result.

5. Gaining publicity – write an article for your local newspaper, trade magazine or any other publication interested in the line of business, hobby or charity supported by your target. Arrange an interview (which can be over the telephone if that is all you can organize) with well-worded prepared questions, a survey or an audit, and record the answers given by your target. Make sure you do not promise publication as this will be out of your control. Write your article with quotes from your target and send a draft copy for approval. Send the article to the various publications and report back to your target on the responses you received.

6. Volunteering – go to your target's charity and offer to help. You do not have to offer regular time – you can offer to help out at special events or projects. It is important your target discovers for themselves that you help and support their charity. If you tell your target you may seem boastful; if someone else mentions it you will endear yourself.

7. Recognising – within your newsletter or blog (you need to produce a regular newsletter or blog and send to your customers and targets) have a section for the biography of special people. You can use this for tactic number 5. Also have sections in your newsletter for the supplier or customer of the month where you can acknowledge your target with a voucher or donation to a charity of their choice.

Tactical strategy 8 – Rewards

An excellent way to get targets on board or to get to meet your target is to offer a reward. Offer vouchers, gifts or financial rewards for referrals or business from referrals. If you set up a referral reward scheme, make it standard and known. The reason for announcing your referral reward scheme is openness, which will make everyone involved feel comfortable and they will not feel they have been used or misled.

The referral reward scheme I introduced was announced in my newsletter and was open to anyone. Often I would be making a payment to a complete stranger (by this I mean I had not spoken to them nor had I had any form of contact with them). How did this work? My newsletter would have found its way into the right hands, who then made connections and recommended my service to someone. I always ask, "How did you hear about my company?" and I would always follow-up no matter how long or convoluted the trail. It always amazed people (especially the hard to trace people) when I told them I wanted to send them a cheque for referring my company's services. This is what I mean by open to everyone.

DIAGNOSTIC QUESTION BOX

What would be a fitting reward to enlist your target?

Eight tips for being a tactical socialiser

1. Go to events, go back again and join – become a member and attend regularly.

2. Direct your energy and focus on one or two people within your target market.

3. Offer to speak at events where your target market will be.

4. Tactically introduce people to each other.

5. Keep in touch – send e-mail on news items, relevant and interesting articles, etc.

6. Do not keep trying to sell your product – you will be asked about it if you build relationships.

7. If you say you will do something then make sure you do it within the time span agreed.

8. Always carry your business cards and give them out.

Tactical socialising should always be fun, even though there is a specific purpose to your socialising and a specific targeted person. If you do not enjoy the chase, capture and moulding of targets, stay at home or get a trusted member of staff to do it, and reward them for each and every target they bring on board. Be generous and generosity will return to you.

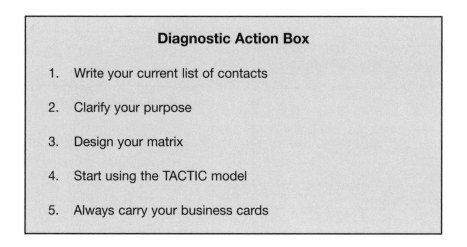

Diagnostic Action Box

1. Write your current list of contacts

2. Clarify your purpose

3. Design your matrix

4. Start using the TACTIC model

5. Always carry your business cards

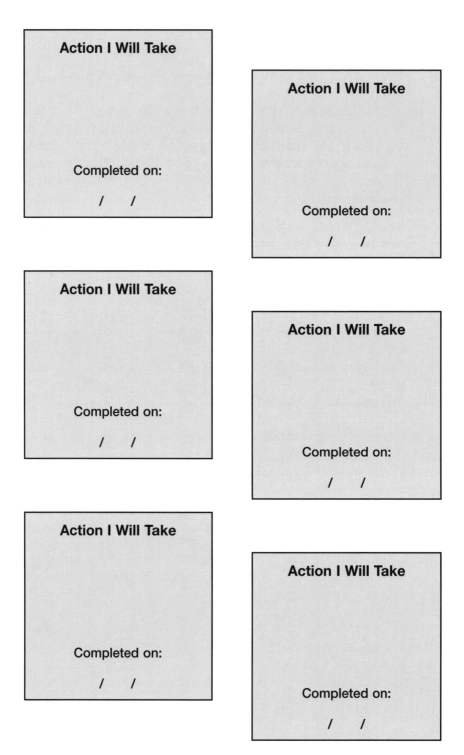

Chapter Eleven

Staff Strategies

The time may come when you need staff to help you cope with your expanding business and to meet and exceed customer service expectations. This chapter highlights some tried and proven strategies that you can use.

Synopsis

Even though you have identified a need for staff, you are not yet at a stage where you need to employ a human resources manager. Here you will discover how to define your 'job and person' profiles, where and when to advertise your vacancies, and the basics of recruitment and selection. Then you are offered valuable insights on keeping your staff aboard and performing at peak productivity.

Although it was in a secondary position, the parade of twenty shops provided an important service to local people, especially the large population of elderly folk who could not easily get to the main town. It had one example of all the usual shops that you might expect in such a place, but for some unknown reason, it had two newsagents.

All the shops were of similar size, with a convenient free car park nearby. One newsagent was part of a national chain and was operated by a manager who lived out of town and was employed by the head office. The other was privately owned and managed by Andrew Walker, a local businessman.

If you were able to see behind the scenes, you would discover some startling differences, especially concerning staffing. Although the chain shop appeared to have the massive advantages of HQ support, training programmes, bulk purchasing power and corporate branding, these all came at a price. There was a 'Group Procedures Manual' that the manager had to strictly follow. He had a tight budget to adhere to and all his stock was determined by the central head office computer, regardless of his customers' local needs. He did, however, have a limited choice on how he used his staff budget. It meant that he could either employ five assistants at the minimum hourly rate or fewer people at a higher wage. Under pressure to meet targets, he opted for the lower paid option.

His shop closed earlier this year, when head office decreed that it was no longer viable and had no place in its future business plan. The true reason for the closure was that the employees were not interested in anything beyond doing the least they could get away with. They were surly, miserable and seemed to perceive customers as annoyances that interfered with their gossip and private mobile phone conversations.

Because they were not motivated, they couldn't be bothered to run the store well. Instead of offering a useful 'opening hours' notice on the door, they plastered the glass with notices: no smoking, no prams, no food or drink, no 'hoodies', only three school children at a time, shoplifters will be prosecuted, we do not give change for telephones, please do not ask for credit as a refusal often offends. These were just the tip of the iceberg that sent potential customers down the road to the privately owned store.

There, because the staff followed the owner's lead and style, they welcomed customers. They were paid well above the minimum rate and had a simple profit-sharing scheme. Although he was an astute businessman, Andrew Walker took time to listen to their ideas and to help when they had personal family problems. Every assistant knew the stock intimately, made suggestions for alternatives if the requested item wasn't available or offered to order it. They took time to greet each customer with a genuine smile and eye contact. They dealt with complaints immediately and courteously. They saw 'the' shop as 'our' shop. When anyone left or went on holiday, they even recommended their friends as replacements and Andrew had a waiting list of good people wanting to join him. His business is a success for him, his staff and his customers.

I asked him for the secret of his success. He replied, "My business is only as good as the weakest member of my staff, which is why I work to have no weak links!"

The day dawns when you decide that you need to employ some-one in your business or that you need to increase your existing staffing levels. Maybe you need to replace someone who is leaving. Before you do any-thing else, you need solid answers to three simple ques-tions: Why do I need some-one? What will their job be? What qualities will the ideal candidate possess? Do not depend on your memory for answers, write them down in as much detail as possible and then go back over them to add or revise as necessary. This is the platform on which your successful staffing strategy depends.

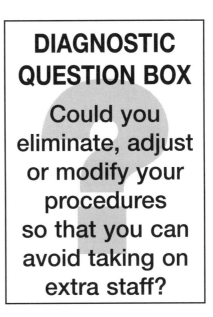

DIAGNOSTIC QUESTION BOX
Could you eliminate, adjust or modify your procedures so that you can avoid taking on extra staff?

Because it is so important to get this stage absolutely right, we need to add some flesh to the bones.

Your answer to, Why do I need someone? will impact on your answers to the other two questions and will help you frame the details.

Typical answers may be: to have more leisure time myself, to allow me more time for administration and marketing, to clear bottle-necks, to improve customer service, to increase turnover and profit, to establish new procedures, to introduce new knowledge into the company, to maintain quality standards ... and you can add to this list according to your situation.

Once you have identified your key primary reason, keep it firmly in mind as you embark on your next two answers. In defining the job, you will actually be laying the ground for a formal job descrip-tion which you will use at the interview stage, and a copy of which will form part of any employment package.

A job description has several components and each must be specified so that both you and your employee know exactly what is expected. In some employment disputes, the job description has played a pivotal role in determining the outcome of legal proceedings. This is not to frighten you, but to stress the importance of this document. At the very minimum, each job description must include the sections listed below. Once you have one version, you can use it as a model for others, so you only need to do the hard work once.

DIAGNOSTIC QUESTION BOX
Does the job description truly reflect your needs and expectations?

Here is the list, which is not in any particular order of priority as each item assumes equal importance:

- Job title
- Place or, if multiple, places of work
- Hours and days of work
- Job share conditions
- Holidays (when, paid, unpaid)
- Maternity and compassionate leave arrangements
- Pay (state conditions for basic, expenses, overtime, pension schemes, bonuses, profit share as appropriate)
- Status (full-time, part-time, hourly wage, weekly wage, monthly salary, self-employed on contract, PAYE tax status, etc.)
- Responsible to – job title of immediate boss (not the name of the person)
- Responsible for – job titles of any subordinates (not the name of the person or persons)
- Tasks (what you expect them to do). Some employers include this text *"and any other tasks that the employer may reasonably expect and that are within your physical capabilities"*.
- Disciplinary procedures (verbal warning, written warning, dismissal, appeals)

- Probationary period
- Appraisal system
- Training available, voluntary or compulsory
- Smoking and drugs policies
- Periods of notice on both sides

To avoid reinventing the wheel, use your favourite internet search engine and see what comes up when you search for job descriptions. You may even find a template that you can use. Another ideas generator could be to review any job description that you or a member of your family have had in the not too distant past. Make any changes needed to reflect your own requirements.

Your final version of the job description should not run to any more than two or three sides of typed A4 paper and, ideally, will have no more than fifteen or twenty topics. For a simple job you will need fewer. If you feel you need more, then consider shifting those that are more generic (non-specific to the job under consideration) to an employee handbook that can be distributed to all your staff.

The nearest relative to the job description is your person profile. Again, begin with a rough draft that you can modify as thoughts come to you and only finalise it as a formal document when you are happy with it. Visualise your ideal person for the job. You could list all the criteria and then, when several candidates apply, use this list as a check sheet for each one. This will clearly not be your only selection tool, but it offers a useful framework.

Here are some ideas for an ideal person list for you to add to, or delete from, according to your job description:

- Gender (where appropriate and legal)
- Experience
- Home location
- Current wage or salary
- Salary expected
- Appearance
- Health
- Intelligence
- Numeric ability

- Literacy
- IT skills
- Other skills
- Team player/leader/member
- Self-starter and self-motivator
- Further education
- Recent education
- Qualifications by examination
- Mobility (car, clean driving licence, valid passport)
- Availability
- Personality
- Family status
- Number of jobs held before
- References
- Criminal record
- Acceptable reasons for leaving last job
- Acceptable reasons for applying for this one

Now that you have your three foundation tools in place, you can enter the potential minefield that is advertising your vacancy. The cheapest option (it is free!) and the safest route is to ask trusted friends, existing staff or relatives if they know of anyone who *might* be interested and to ask them to get in touch with you. Personal recommendation is the best reference of all. Remember you should always interview and take up references regardless of any referrals.

DIAGNOSTIC QUESTION BOX

Does this person exist outside of your imagination?

For skilled, specialist or managerial posts, you can save yourself a lot of time and possible hassle by using an employment agency, but be prepared to pay them a commission of around ten to thirty per cent of the proposed first year salary. For unskilled and semi-skilled workers, your local Job Centre may have suitable candidates as their clients, and their services are free. The Job Centre should also be able to provide you with guidance notes on recruitment and employment law. These will help you if you decide to advertise. The three key words to remember when planning any situations vacant advertising are where, when and what.

You have placed your advertisement, you have received some replies (which you have checked against your ideal person list) and you will have shortlisted any potential candidates. Their presentation can often reveal more than the words they use. If you suspect they have used the paper, envelopes and franking machine of their current employer, then question their honesty and integrity! If they have sent what is obviously a standard letter that has gone out to dozens of possible employers, question their seriousness and dedication in writing to you. Other warning signs might include spelling and basic grammar errors, obvious ignorance of the correct layout of letters, getting your name wrong, lack of a date and even contradictions in their text.

Next you invite them for an interview. Before a single word is exchanged you will notice, and maybe even record, marks out of ten for punctuality, dress, cleanliness, general presentation and facial expression, especially important if your applicant will be greeting your customers face to face.

There are some things that you cannot do or ask in an interview. You are forbidden by law to ask questions about age, race, gender, sexual orientation or disabilities. You are not allowed to ask females of any age about their pregnancy plans, even though these could cost you dearly in maternity pay and replacement cover. It is safest to have (and then keep on file) a list of questions that you stick to for every candidate. This way you can be seen to be demonstrably fair and you will make your own comparison tasks easier.

You must never make personal remarks or observations and you must not harass or bully. Limit your remarks to the job on offer. In this age of litigation, it is always wise for a male interviewer to have a female observer present as a chaperone when interviewing female staff. This is simple protection against any potential false claims of harassment or impropriety, and it offers another person's views on the applicant which you may have missed.

You can ask about their present and expected salary or wage. It is useful to note that your staff budget must cover more than wages. You will probably need to add a third to the bottom line salary figure to cover your on-costs like National Insurance payments, employer's liability insurance, professional indemnity and public liability insurance, PAYE administration. You may also need to include costs of recruitment and selection procedures and possible sick leave or maternity leave cover.

It can be a long journey from "hello and welcome" to "farewell, thanks and enjoy your retirement". In the vast majority of cases it will also be a happy one for all concerned. However, you need to have strategies in place for dealing with poor performance, misdemeanours, serious breaches of conduct and, of course, departures.

With very few exceptions, the law states that each employee must be provided with a contract of employment and (although not always enshrined in law) copies of any other related documents, such as procedures manuals, policy manuals, pension documentation, health and safety conditions and disciplinary procedures.

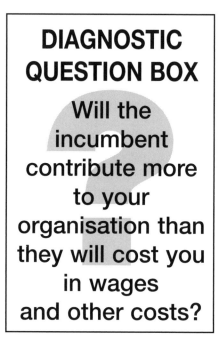

DIAGNOSTIC QUESTION BOX

Will the incumbent contribute more to your organisation than they will cost you in wages and other costs?

The contract of employment can be a pretty standard document which you can customise for each employee. For example, it should state if any trial period or probationary period elapses before any other clauses concerning period of notice come into effect.

In some circumstances you will need a formal induction and training procedure and you should ensure that any existing staff are co-operative and involved with this. Apart from your approach to any day-to-day encounters with your staff, one of the best tools for ensuring that you run 'a tight but happy ship' is the annual, bi-annual or quarterly staff appraisal. This is a designated period of an hour or so, which you set aside for a closely focused one-to-one dialogue with an individual employee.

Appraisal

The appraisal begins with the good news about achievements, successes, compliance with suggestions from any previous appraisals and honest input from your employee about how well they think they have done. Always be positive during this phase and offer encouragement and praise where it is due. If an employee is not performing to previously agreed standards in a certain area of their work, invite the employee to speak about it in the next phase.

The middle phase is where you have to suspend judgment and criticism as you ask the employee to tell you 'like it is' from their viewpoint. Stay in control, but let them unload any problems, complaints, fears or worries. Do not accept vague statements that can have no solution, like "I feel demotivated." Ask where, when, why and how they feel this way. Your objective is to reveal specific issues so that lasting solutions can be found.

The middle phase is also where, working together, the two of you set out plans, objectives or goals for the coming year. A goal without a time frame is just a wish, so set dates for the start and completion of each planned activity, so that both of you have milestones against which to measure progress.

Finally, write an appraisal report which summarises your discussion and give a copy to the employee involved. Then allow the employee a day or three to consider the contents (be prepared to make any fair and agreed changes) then ask them to sign and date it. Keep a copy for yourself and give the employee a copy so that you both have a permanent reminder and a start point for the next appraisal.

Conflict Resolution

Seek reasons for your employee defaulting and consider possible solutions first and only take disciplinary action later if needed. Conflict can erupt spontaneously in any workplace. If not acted upon in the early stages it can become as endemic as a malignant cancer. In many situations it cannot be resolved with ease but might be with the seven Es.

Your first 'E' is to *Establish* the facts. You can act on facts; you are pretty powerless to do anything about opinion, gossip, hearsay, feelings or other non-specifics.

Your next 'E' is to call all the parties concerned (individually at first, then together) so that you can *Explain* the situation as you see it from the facts. Then you *Express* how you feel about it, *Elicit* their views and state the *Exact* behaviour that you require. As the steel fist within your velvet glove, define the *Eventual* consequences of failure to create and sustain *Exemplary* behaviour.

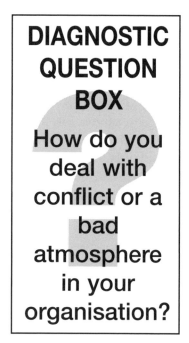

DIAGNOSTIC QUESTION BOX

How do you deal with conflict or a bad atmosphere in your organisation?

The majority of staff can be expected to conduct themselves properly at work. Here are some of the areas where conflict can arise: persistent lateness, harassment, unauthorised absence, breaches of house rules, poor performance, fighting at work and inappropriate conduct. Any offender has the potential to damage your business, reduce the morale of other staff and upset customers so, as a caring employer, you need an early warning system based on your intuition, observation and a sharp eye and keen ear on the gossip grapevine. In every case you must determine the facts and keep detailed written records of any events.

Your disciplinary procedures must be written, available to all staff and rigorously followed. The typical sequence is two or three verbal warnings, followed by two or three written warnings, followed by dismissal. Again, record keeping is vitally important. After each warning meeting you must make a written report of all that was agreed, including the date of the meeting and measurements for the improvement required, and both you and the employee must date and sign it.

Some myths about what you cannot do are just that – myths. Here are some myths:

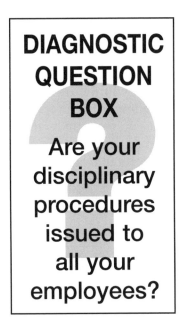

DIAGNOSTIC QUESTION BOX

Are your disciplinary procedures issued to all your employees?

- *I cannot contact a sick employee.* Employers have the right to know how an employee is progressing during their absence and to have some indication of how long the absence might last.

- *I cannot sack an employee who is off sick.* Provided you consult with the employee, obtain medical reports and possibly look at adjustments to their job or consider alternative work, and consult with professional legal advisors, it is possible.

- *I have to advertise internally.* There is no law at present that states this.

- *I must let Muslims pray on demand.* There is a period of about two hours in the middle of the day when Muslims must pray so, provided they are allowed to pray sometime during this period, it is unlikely that you would fall foul of any religious discrimination legislation.

Suppose one of your employees decides that they want to leave and hands you a letter to this effect. You will keep this letter in your staff files for completeness and any possible future reference.

Although it is by no means universal, many employers attach as much importance to an exit interview as they do to recruitment interviews. When a person decides to leave and you have arranged mutually acceptable terms, they have nothing to lose by telling you the truth about their time with you and their reasons for going. This interview may well reveal problems and frictions that you were unaware of, personality clashes, unfair procedures, uneven distribution of workload, adverse working conditions, unacceptable ambience and similar issues.

The well conducted exit interview can help to ensure that the employee leaves you with a good impression about your business, so that they will not be tempted to bad-mouth you to anyone and thus damage your reputation or erode goodwill. You will find it useful to have an exit checklist to use. If departures are regular events, reference to completed lists and interview notes will help you spot trends and to take corrective action. Your exit list could include:

- Employee name
- Job title
- Department
- Stated reasons for leaving
- Suspected true reasons for leaving
- Length of service
- New employer
- Date of resignation letter
- Agreed termination date
- Your own notes and observations at the time

Again, you should keep this document and answers on file. You may never need to refer to it again, but there are instances when the police or other authorities may need to seek information about ex-employees.

Your successor as an employer may seek references from you. The reference you give must be honest, fair and not misleading or malicious, and refer to facts the employee knew about. Keep a copy of any references that you give. If you cannot give a good reference, stick to only the facts you can back up with evidence from disciplinary or attendance records.

Let me end this chapter with a final cautionary thought or two. As an employer you have personal responsibility for complying with the requirements of HM Revenue and Customs, National Insurance, immigration status and employment law, so make sure you are fully informed and take appropriate legal advice before taking action which might result in you being taken to court or being invited to an employment tribunal.

Diagnostic Action Box

1. Consider all alternatives before increasing your staff levels

2. Write a job description and an ideal person profile

3. Use the Es strategy for conflict resolution

4. Adhere to defined and published disciplinary procedures

5. Conduct exit interviews

6. Seek legal advice promptly

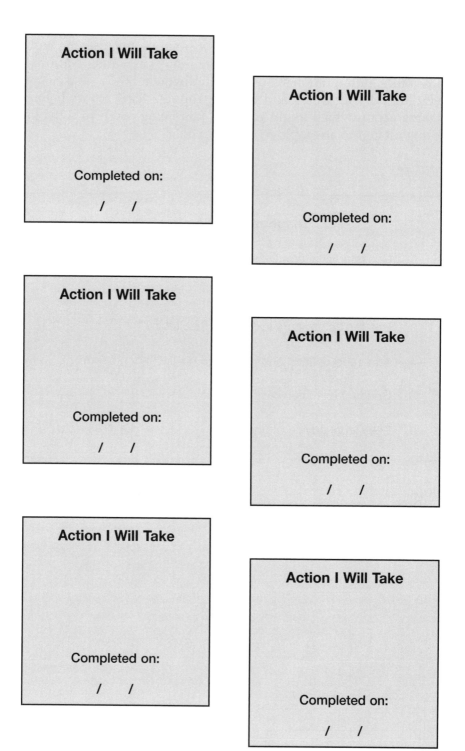

Action I Will Take

Completed on:

/   /

Action I Will Take

Completed on:

/   /

Action I Will Take

Completed on:

/   /

Action I Will Take

Completed on:

/   /

Action I Will Take

Completed on:

/   /

Action I Will Take

Completed on:

/   /

Chapter Twelve

Challenge Resolution

Every challenge, in every business, in every country, is eventually resolved, therefore a problem is not a problem until you make it one: call it a challenge instead.

Synopsis

This chapter is about dealing with challenges, about turning mountains into molehills and molehills into flat plains of smooth endeavour. There has probably never been a business that has not had its share of challenges. The unprepared go under – which is still a solution of sorts. The coached business owner uses challenges to build a stronger business than before, like the landlord in our opening story.

The public house had stood in the centre of the market square for over 250 years. It was virtually unchanged but it had seen many changes happen around it. Originally it was a coaching inn on an unmade road in a small village on a popular pilgrimage route. Apart from the church opposite, it was the largest building in those days. It had never suffered a fire, nobody had ever been killed or injured in it and the ever-changing menu had never poisoned anyone.

Eventually, progress almost defeated it. The road had been surfaced and the oil lamps were replaced, first with gas and then electricity. The village green became a car park and the village grew into a small town, but the inn retained its former character. It was a popular meeting place for locals and tourists alike. It had retained its independence and survived by providing good, honest accommodation and meals that were famous for miles around. Then the 'men in suits' came.

Although it had never had a fire, the current landlord Stan Gibbs was required to spend a small fortune on fire precautions and subject his premises to an annual fire certificate inspection – or be closed down. Although nobody had ever been killed or injured, the accommodation had to comply with the recommendations of an annual health and safety check. Although nobody had ever been poisoned, the kitchens had to be open to random inspections by public health officials.

Stan accepted these additional burdens, wrote the cheques for the inspections, maintained the policy manuals and certificates and got on with his business. Then the various rules and regulations were modified. This led to a business challenge which threatened to end the pub's commercial viability.

The rear of the kitchen was slightly below ground level because the building was on a small hill. There was a window on the wall at ground level, which kept the chef cool and sane in the warmth of summer and allowed any condensation from cooking to escape, just as it had for two-and-a-half centuries.

"That window is a health hazard," said the public health man. "It must be bricked up – or else!" "That window is part of your fire escape route," said the fireman. "It must be kept with clear access at all times – or else!" The health and safety inspector said, "It is too big – people could fall in from outside. Reduce its size by seventy-five per cent – or else!" To complete the landlord's dilemma, the heritage people who had listed the building said, "You must not change the external appearance, including that window – or else!"

Stan was inventive at solving business challenges; he found a solution that satisfied all the men in suits, and one that still allowed an opening big enough for his rotund chef to escape.

The chef was delighted with this new slim-line shelf unit that allowed him to store and retrieve his jars of spices. He had not even noticed that it had a steel back and was exactly the same size as the window beside it. That is where the rack stayed most of the time, even during the fireman's visit. He had not even paid any attention to the runners above and below the window frame that allowed the shelf unit to slide across, and totally conceal the window from within, when the other 'suits' made their annual visits.

The external appearance did not change, except for the planting of a large bush that hid the window from any prying eyes or potential intruders in the garden. Stan said, "I couldn't face the challenge head-on and satisfy all the authorities. So I did what anyone could do – instead of going over or under the challenge, I just went around it."

It is often said that 'a problem shared is a problem halved'. It is more motivating to say that, 'a challenge defined is a challenge solved'. As soon as you define a challenge from every angle, you can establish its size, scope and potential for disaster. Better still, you can examine all the options towards resolving it.

There is an earlier preliminary step. You may think that you have a challenge but if your clients, suppliers, staff and business associates do not believe that there is one, then you had better examine your conscience and see if it exists in reality. It may only exist in your own mind. Attempting to resolve a challenge that does not exist will only create one.

If you suspect that you have a real challenge, write it down in simple words – the fewer the better. A short pencil is better than a long memory, and the act of writing is the first step towards identifying your challenge. Write as many different descriptions as you need until you reach one that describes the challenge most accurately and in the briefest format. Now transfer this version to the top of a fresh sheet of paper and place it aside. You will return to it later.

As you work on this editing task, ask yourself these questions.

DIAGNOSTIC QUESTION BOX

What type of challenge is it?

- Is this situation of my own causing and is it down to me to do something about it? Think of this as a 'me' challenge. For example, if your business financial outgoings exceed your income.

- Is this situation a result of the actions of someone else and can I do anything about it? Think of this as a 'them' challenge. For example, if a member of staff has a personal hygiene problem, or new government regulations are introduced that will adversely affect your business.
- Is this situation a result of something way beyond my control and how can I minimize its impact? Think of this as a 'universe' challenge. For example, floods, wars, earthquakes, forest fires, tidal waves, terrorist attacks.

You can, and should, deal with the 'me' and 'them' challenges as soon as possible, because if you leave them alone and trust to luck that they will go away, they will simply grow and beget further challenges. Those in the 'universe' category are best catered for by good insurance cover.

As soon as possible does not mean a knee-jerk reaction, it means taking as long as it takes to decide on your actions, and then implementing them.

When you are in the middle of a dense forest it is impossible to get your bearings. When you climb a tall tree you gain a clearer perspective. If it was possible to rise to an altitude of 500 feet in a helicopter you would know exactly where you are; rise to 20,000 feet in a pressurised aircraft and you may not even see the forest at all.

The point of this analogy is that distance adds clarity. Before you make any action decisions, put a space between yourself and the challenge. This may mean taking a walk around the block, an away day at your nearest beach or, perhaps, a trip to the theatre or a restaurant. As soon as you add distance by doing something different, you will find it easier to see the size and implications of the challenge and be able to select from the many options that are available to you.

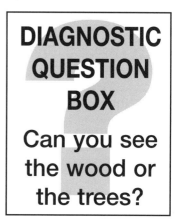

DIAGNOSTIC QUESTION BOX

Can you see the wood or the trees?

A note of caution is due here. You will notice that I have referred to 'the challenge' and not, 'the challenges'. It is relatively simple to resolve one challenge when you use this process. It is very difficult to solve two or more simultaneously. If, at this stage, you feel that you do have more than one challenge, just prioritise them, then deal with the most immediate one first. You may well find that this reduces the complexity and number of the other challenges.

When you have selected your key challenge, written it down, asked the questions and stepped back a pace or six, you are ready for the next sequence of actions.

If your challenge is small enough to explain and understand with a one-minute verbal description, you can press right ahead to the sequence below.

If your challenge is larger than this, you need to dilute it or 'chunk it down'. This simply means that you break it down into a series of related elements, so that you can find a solution to each element in isolation, and then build all the solutions back together at the end. Recalling the story that opened this chapter, our landlord had a single challenge with a window. It was partly a 'me' challenge but had huge elements of 'them' in it too. By chunking down to what was needed to satisfy each of the men in suits in turn, he was able to create a win-win situation.

Beware the tempting trap of dealing with the symptoms of your challenge rather than its cause or causes. Symptom sorting can be a quick fix but it will not resolve the challenge. It is a bit like pulling the head off a weed and leaving the roots in the ground. Eventually the challenge, like the weed, will surface again, possibly stronger than ever.

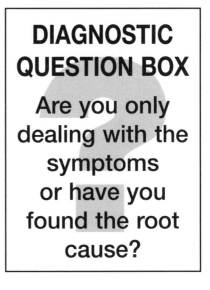

DIAGNOSTIC QUESTION BOX

Are you only dealing with the symptoms or have you found the root cause?

Return now to your paper with its simple definition of the challenge. Work on answering these questions in sequence and write down brief notes:

What are the symptoms?	Think of the results that made you aware of the challenge
Are these significant issues?	If not, then maybe you do not really have a challenge
What are the causes?	Work back to the initial prime cause
Where was it caused?	Consider all possibilities
Who caused it?	Work back to the initial prime cause
When was it caused?	This may be much earlier than the apparent symptoms
Why was it caused?	The events, actions or omissions that created it

The first step to defeating any enemy is to gain as much knowledge as you can, and the same is true of dealing with a challenge. When you have worked through the seven questions above, you will have a far clearer understanding of your challenge.

Again, take a break and then return to review your notes, adding, deleting or modifying as needed. As soon as you believe that you have as much clarity as possible, you are ready for the next critical examination. Although it may seem like repetition, the repetition will help you understand the situation fully.

Take another sheet of paper and write your answers to the following questions:

What was done – or not done?	Brief and simple is the key
What could have been done – or not done?	Consider all options

What should have been done – or not done?	Select the best solution
Why that particular action?	Note your reason
What action is needed to resolve?	When will you take it?
Who was involved?	Name all parties
Who else could have been involved?	Think 'who could help?'
Who should have been involved?	Select the best person
Why that person?	Note your reason
What action is needed to resolve?	When will you take it?
When did it happen?	Specify dates
When could it have happened?	Was it always a threat?
When should it have happened?	'Not at all' is an OK reply
Why then?	What differences would it have made?
What action is needed to resolve?	When will you take it?
Where did it happen?	Home, work, somewhere else?
Where could it have happened?	Anywhere, be specific
Where should it have happened?	Define a location
Why there?	Note your reasons
What action is needed to resolve?	When will you take it?
Why did it happen?	Do not seek to blame
Why else could it have happened?	Any other reasons?
Why else should it happen?	Think creatively
Why that?	Give specific reasons
What action is needed to resolve?	When will you take it?

It is impossible to say how long this process will take. For a simple challenge you may be looking at an hour or so. For a more complex one, it may take several days spread over a few weeks. Your sole objective is gathering as much information as you can about the cause of your challenge. When you have completed the sequence, you will have five answers to 'What action is needed to resolve it?'

DIAGNOSTIC QUESTION BOX

Have you skipped any of the above questions? Left the root still in the ground?

Now ascertain whether you can actually take these actions to resolve the challenge by checking that none of them rules out any of the others, that each will make the situation better rather than worse, and ensuring that they are within your abilities, capabilities and responsibilities.

There is just one more stage to go through. Take five new sheets of paper and write across the top of each piece one of the 'actions needed to resolve'. Your final stage is to take an inventory of your resources as you consider these questions against each of the five sheets in turn:

Who else do you need to involve?	To provide any knowledge that you lack
What else do you need to acquire?	Funds, skills, materials, time, etc.
Where else will you need to go?	Libraries, internet, professional practitioners
When will you be able to act?	Specific start dates
When will the issue be closed?	Specific target dates

When you reach this point you will be well-equipped to deal with virtually any challenge that may beset your business or, indeed, your personal life. In my experience the commonest business challenges usually involve partnerships and finances. (Business partnership can be as fraught, or as perfect, as a marriage.)

It was Winston Churchill who stated that "to jaw-jaw is always better than to war-war", so when you consider your actions remember the importance of talking with all parties concerned to seek mutually acceptable solutions. Do not try to apportion blame, including any form of self blame, because it serves absolutely no purpose and achieves nothing. Remind yourself that you always learn more from adversity than you do from smooth sailing. However, do not seek to be adversarial.

A business coach may well prove to be your biggest help. With no hidden agenda and no involvement with any of the personalities, with no stake in the outcome beyond your satisfaction, your coach can take a more distant and wide-angled view of a situation so that he or she will help you to 'see the wood from the trees'.

There has never yet been a challenge that was not capable of being resolved. Yours will be too when you use this chapter as a starting point.

Diagnostic Action Box

1. Ensure the challenge exists

2. Chunk down and deal with the chunks

3. Deal with one challenge at a time

4. Gather as much information as possible before coming to conclusions

5. Identify and assemble the resources you need to resolve the challenge

6. Take action to resolve it!

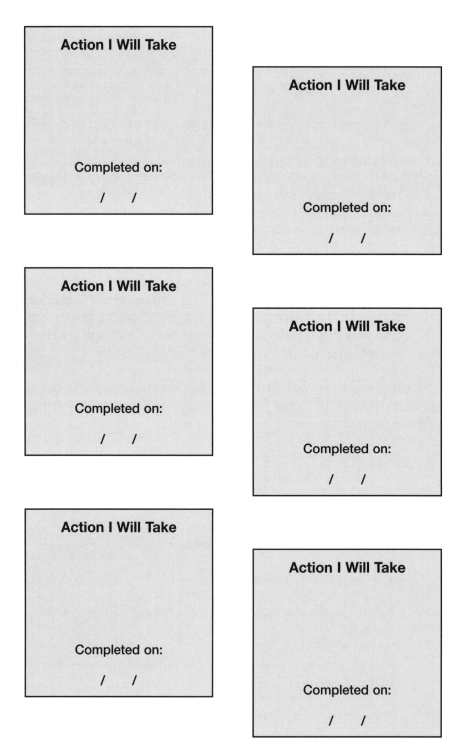

Action I Will Take

Completed on:

/ /

Action I Will Take

Completed on:

/ /

Action I Will Take

Completed on:

/ /

Action I Will Take

Completed on:

/ /

Action I Will Take

Completed on:

/ /

Action I Will Take

Completed on:

/ /

Chapter Thirteen

Money Matters

No business can thrive, develop or create jobs and profits unless some fundamental financial factors are carefully considered.

Synopsis

You would be amazed how many entrepreneurs and directors fight shy of doing their sums. That is possibly why accountancy is such a successful industry. As one accountant put it: "This can be a grotty job, but someone has to do it." But, of course, an accountant can only report on the facts that have already happened. To ensure that no nasty surprises are revealed, the buck stops with you and your preparation. This chapter offers an insight into the most perilous pitfalls of sales value, margins, costs and cash flow.

Alice Harding, a management consultant, had been on the assignment for a month. She had almost completed her initial tour of the various departments and premises of a well-known supplier of nursery products. She was surprised at some of the facts she had uncovered. She was even more surprised to return to the HQ offices to find a party in full swing. They were celebrating confirmation of a massive order to supply the company's new, revolutionary high chair, which easily converted for many other uses in the home and car. Not wishing to be a party-pooper she went along with the fun but as soon as possible, she made her excuses and left.

The next morning she sought an urgent meeting with the managing director of the group. She immediately broke her news. "Instead of a party last night, you should have been holding a wake! That big new order could even be the end of the company. You are already losing £2 on every one of these chairs that you sell and, because of the discounts you have given to secure this order, this loss could rise to £5 per unit."

In the stunned silence that followed, the managing director opened his folder, hitting each section with the back of his hand as he turned it. "Last year's figures! Every department from administration to maintenance has achieved or exceeded their targets. Sales, marketing, accounts, distribution, purchasing, manufacturing – they are all on target. The repairs and servicing department has even expanded and shifted more product than ever before."

The consultant nodded. "I agree, but there are two big problems. Each department *is* performing well but with little or no inter-relationship with the others. And the service department is the biggest offender. For two weeks last month, they actually received more chairs for repair under guarantee than you sold. Carry on like this and you might as well skip the sales process and take them direct from factory to repair shop!"

The company did not go under but this overlooked aspect of integrated financial control and erroneous pricing meant the loss of a factory and jobs in a depressed area of Britain. To contain costs, components were manufactured in China and the once proud factory simply became an assembly and packing shop. All because the sums did not add up and nobody had spotted it in time.

Just because you are great at running your business, it does not automatically follow that you are great at controlling the sums. In this chapter you are invited to consider the flow of cash, and I promise not to flood you with a deluge of accountancy jargon. Instead, think of your enterprise as being like a pump where you feed time, processes and money in at one end, so that it delivers profit at the other end.

Let us begin with sales value, which is joined at the hip with your prices. In this context, price means the actual cost to your customer, whether this is a fee for professional services or payment for goods. If you set your price too low, your business will have a short life. Set them too high and your competitors will steal your clients or you will have a low volume of sales.

If you are already in business, disregard your current prices for a moment and imagine that you are just starting from scratch. Find three competitors offering similar services to yours. Look for one at the top end of your market, one at the cheapest end and the one that you perceive as being the biggest player. Check their products or services and find the one that most closely corresponds to your own main products or services.

Make a note of all three prices. Now write your planned price for the same output. If it is higher than the most expensive, you must be able to justify the premium price. If it is lower than the cheapest, ask why you are prepared to work for less. If it is around the mid-point, you are probably on the right track. You can always change your prices for new customers later but for now, head for the middle market. Here is a simple example: if you work in male hairdressing, you

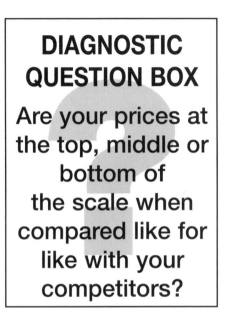

DIAGNOSTIC QUESTION BOX

Are your prices at the top, middle or bottom of the scale when compared like for like with your competitors?

could find that the most expensive cut costs around £200, because the premises are in Mayfair and the top stylist regularly appears on television make-over shows and in magazine articles as 'stylist to the stars'. The cheapest may be that traditional owner-managed barber shop in a rarely visited corner of town. He has been in business for thirty years and charges £5 for a basic haircut. A quick check of prices for all the other barbers and hairdressers in your area indicates an average of £20. As a starting point, aim for this average price.

In every instance the time taken to cut a client's hair is going to be much the same. The only variable as far as the client is concerned is the ambience and the result. However, as far as you are concerned, there are more variables and these include your costs and profit margins.

This is where the concept of value arises. You must set your prices to reflect the expectations and values of your client, not your own sense of value. A hypnotherapist told me: "I feel really uncomfortable asking £50 for a consultation; after all, it only takes an hour of my time." I reminded her of her investment in training, her acquired knowledge, experience and the costs of her premises, advertising, insurance and the level of fees charged by other therapists in her area. She was a lovely person, but was guilty of pricing according to her own sense of value, rather than the value her clients perceived and received from her services. After our conversation she increased her fee to £70 per forty-five minute session and lost her feelings of guilt while gaining income. A small step in the right direction.

Price your goods or services according to the benefits, perceived or real, they deliver to your clients.

There are other ingredients that must be factored into the pricing mix. In the example of our hypnotherapist, there are income limits because her available time is limited. She can only work effectively for eight hours a day and for six days a week. To increase her volume of clients, and thus her income, she would have to employ someone to work for her and that is going to come with extra costs. The only place this cost can be recovered is through higher fees. The most obvious solution is to add a 'higher perceived value' option to her portfolio of services. Another way is to sell her expertise by running training courses, selling products like CDs and books, or even expand her brand awareness by offering franchises for a fee.

Another ingredient in your price/value calculation is your profit margin.

If your product or service costs thousands of pounds, you will not sell in high volumes and your profit margin will reflect this. Cars, yachts, aircraft, machinery, executive consultancy, cameras, research and most luxury goods fall into this category.

On the other hand, if your product or service is aimed at high volume, low cost sales, your profit on each one will be tiny – think of all the items found in your local 'Everything £1' shop, newspapers and so on. The more expensive your products or services, the higher you must set your profit margin.

So how do you set a fair profit margin for your time or goods?

Remember that you are, to some extent, limited by market pressures and the prices being charged by your competitors. I wonder if you have spotted the way around this? It is to create a unique product or service that has no competitors. Another way is to create a unique angle on an existing business by doing things differently or by making your product different in some way.

There is a company that sells household tool kits consisting of a hammer, pliers, torch and a few other bits and pieces. They have low overheads because they sell their goods only on the internet and yet they charge premium prices. These are justified by aiming their kits at the female market and everything, including the box, is painted in shocking rock-candy bright pink. This ensures that men are unlikely to want to wander off with the tools, and creates an instant sales appeal for gift buyers who are stuck with what to buy for the woman who has almost everything.

A wedding photographer charges competitive prices for his basic service but then offers the bride, groom and immediate family a digitally produced glossy magazine of the event, complete with captions, just like the popular 'celebrity glossy' publications. This is such a contrast to the traditional album of prints that he can charge a premium price and create significant profits.

How to calculate profit

There is no single profit calculation formula that applies to all businesses, but a useful starting point is to consider all your costs multiplied by four.

Thus, of the price that your customer pays:

A. Twenty-five per cent is for your goods, raw materials, time and production processes

B. Twenty-five per cent is for your overheads and other costs

C. Twenty-five per cent is for contingencies

D. Twenty-five per cent is your profit

We could play with these figures and fill the rest of this book with worked examples but, instead, as we consider each of them in turn, think about how they apply to your situation.

Component A is pretty self-evident but it is important to ensure that you include ALL of your costs. The story that opened this chapter reveals how things can go sour, because the company had treated its repair and service department as a net contributor rather than a cost. If your first working of these sums makes your selling price unacceptable (to you or your clients) then seek ways of reducing your Component A costs. This could be through negotiating better deals with your suppliers, asking for a sale or return arrangement or even finding new suppliers. Would an investment in new or bet-

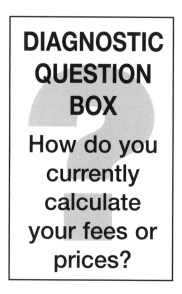

DIAGNOSTIC QUESTION BOX

How do you currently calculate your fees or prices?

ter tools reduce time? If you create scrap as a by-product, could this be sold?

As an example, a major UK supplier of timber buildings now bales all its sawdust and chippings and sells them as horse stable bedding. This company makes a very good profit from something that it would otherwise have to pay to be taken away.

Component B is all your other costs that do not fit into 'A'. These include the on-costs that would still be there even if you did nothing in your business: rent, council tax, insurances, telephones, back office computers, utilities bills, mortgages, bank loans, overdrafts, credit cards, professional accountants or advisers. There are few established businesses that could not shave a few percentages off here. If you are in a high cost location but do not really need to be, think about relocating to a cheaper position, looking for grants to help you, consolidating expensive credit into a more affordable loan arrangement, reducing the numbers of vehicles that you run – and always buying second-hand vehicles to avoid the massive first year depreciation on new ones, or consider leasing cars and expensive equipment.

A seaside gems, rocks and fossils business was able to slash its Component B costs by selling the freehold of its seasonal shop and then renting back the stockroom, from which it ran an internet-based mail order company. To retain a retail presence in the town, they rented space within a nearby gift shop for the twelve weeks of summer.

Component C is where you expect the unexpected. As a general rule, you will always over-estimate your profits and under-estimate your costs. This seems to be human nature. If you have no Component C you will be up the proverbial creek if you hit a snag. Maybe the roof of your premises is damaged by a storm and you need immediate repairs before the insurance company pays out a pitiful percentage of your claim. Perhaps you are ill and need to hire someone to cover for you.

The safety net of Component C is like arranging your own insurance. Put it into a high interest, instant access savings account and do not be tempted to use it to top-up your day-to-day expenses. If, hopefully, at the end of the year you find that you have not used this component, then congratulate yourself. There is no point in seeking to reduce Component C – indeed, if anything, you should look to increase it!

Component D is the only reason for starting and running any business. Whatever reductions you can make at A and B will have a positive impact on D. Alas, the reverse is equally true if you increase A and B, although the impact will then be negative. Profit is where you pay yourself – and you MUST pay yourself first. If your cash flow does not allow this, then you have no option but to return to the drawing board and repeat all your calculations, then change what needs to be changed so that you can pay yourself.

If you have an issue with the pursuit of profit to the extent where you find the whole concept mildly immoral or 'gaining at the expense of others', do bear in mind that another word for profit is freedom. Once you have your freedom funds (profit) you can do what you wish with them. Use them for good works, to subsidise fees to clients who need your services but cannot afford the full price, or even give them away. Whatever keeps your conscience clear! But do not dispose of all of your profits.

A good rule of thumb is to allocate your profits four ways. The exact proportions will, of course, depend on your lifestyle, so think in percentage terms that are appropriate to you. You clearly need to use some to meet your personal expenses (apart from the business costs already discussed). These will include your home, utilities, food, clothing and other essentials. It is a good idea to set some aside in a 'rainy day' interest bearing account, and a similar amount in another account that you can use to develop or establish your next business. As for the rest, have fun and enjoy it, you have earned it!

Julian and Tina Sprigs ran a successful seaside guest house. Despite being on call 24/7 they were happy, until a helpful guest pointed out that they were paying themselves less than half the legal minimum hourly wage. They did the types of sums outlined in this chapter, put the guest house on the market and bought a shop instead!

You will sometimes hear a successful, wealthy tycoon brag that he or she 'did it all on OPM' which is their jargon for 'other people's money'. Whether these 'other people' are investors, banks, friends, associates or simply your wealthy old auntie, remember that they can ask for it back at any time, usually with interest. With OPM you are restricting your freedom, as these stakeholders may well want a say in how you run your business. But unless you inherit funds, win a lottery or were born rich, you will almost certainly have to borrow some start-up funds.

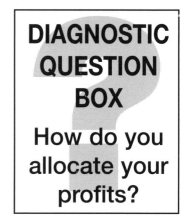

DIAGNOSTIC QUESTION BOX

How do you allocate your profits?

So far I have discussed the flow of money in and the flood, typically, of money out. So almost without noticing it and certainly without jargon, we come to cash flow matters. Your accountant and tax man will need standard profit and loss accounts but may not require or request cash flow details. However, if your bank does not ask for cash flow forecasts, YOU need them. They do not have to be complicated. Many banks or Business Link-type agencies can even give you free forms to make it easy.

On paper, and in reality, cash flow must be monitored and measured against two criteria. The first is your 'cash flow forecast' where you predict the next 12 months. If this veers too far towards creative fiction, you will have a nasty shock when you create the second form with identical headings. This will be 'actual cash flow' and if it differs too far from the forecast, you had better have some darned good answers ready to explain the differences. Make regular comparisons between the two to see how close you are to your forecast.

The simplest format for these documents is where you have twelve vertical columns, one for each month of the year. On the left-hand side you list every outgoing business cost you can imagine, and then you fill in the totals for each month. Draw a line and similarly list all your sources of business income, month by month, according to expected volumes of sales. Add a thirteenth column for running totals across the page.

For each month you then subtract the outgoings from the income to show how much cash you have available that month. If you have to subtract income from outgoings, you will have a minus figure as your cash is flowing the wrong way – right into the red.

These cash flow documents are not indicators of profit or loss. They are simply your measurement of funds in your bank accounts. It is worth remembering that you can spend profit (subject to my cautions above), but you must never spend turnover. Unless you manage your money, your eventual lack of money will manage you. Your cash flow documents will help you plan when, during the year, you can consider significant investments or expansion for your business during the year.

I end this chapter with one very simple golden rule. If you keep track of your business and personal accounting daily, it will take a few minutes per day. Do it weekly and it will take an hour or two. Leave the periods any longer and you will eventually need to devote entire days to doing the sums. They will not go away. Like wire coat hangers in a wardrobe, they will seemingly increase and multiply spontaneously until they become a tangled mess that attacks you whenever you open the door.

You must bite the bullet, grasp the nettle, face your fears or whatever other metaphor you prefer. The sooner you do it, the easier it is.

Finally, keep your fingers out of the till! For every £1 that you 'borrow' you will have to turn over at least £4 to put it back.

IMPORTANT NOTE: This chapter contains the author's opinions based on her experience. It is not qualified accountancy advice so must not be used as such. In all matters of financial decisions or legal matters, you must always seek appropriate professional advice.

Diagnostic Action Box

1. Check your fees and prices against competitors

2. Regularly review costs and seek reductions

3. Avoid spending your profits and never spend your turnover

4. Create a cash flow forecast for comparison with actual cash flow

5. Deal with financial matters in small regular sessions – daily or weekly

---

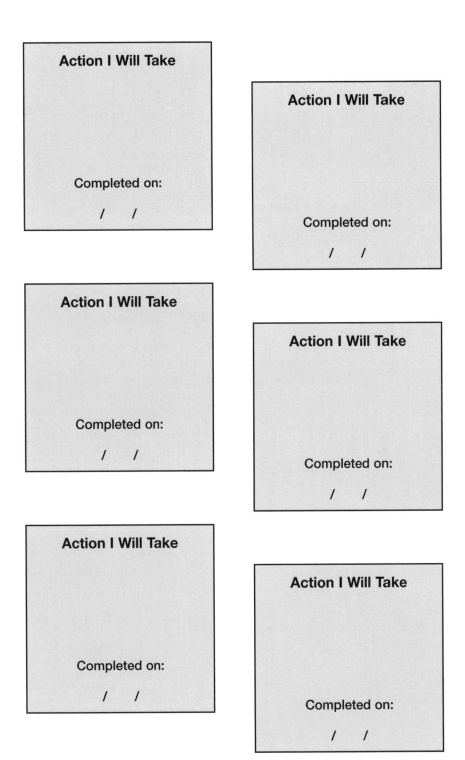

Chapter Fourteen

Money from Waste

Where there is muck there is money – only this time you do not have to get dirty.

Synopsis

There is always waste to be found in any business and this chapter looks at a variety of areas where you can save money or increase profit by looking at what you do and how you do it. Read on and you will discover areas of waste you may have never considered.

Julie Bond has worked in the garment industry for many years and knows her job inside out. She is considered by her bosses to be a hard-working and conscientious employee. Over the years Julie has been promoted from the shop floor to the pattern office. Today is her first day on her own (she received one day of training from a disgruntled and hassled supervisor) and she is now responsible for producing the paper patterns for all the new designs.

She selects the garment design from the production plans, looks at the separate pattern cuts that are needed to make up each design and then organises the printing of the patterns on to the material prior to cut-out. Julie feels a little apprehensive but has been trained and has also been with the company for so long that she does not want to appear stupid by asking for further help. Everyone else is very busy and they do not want to be bothered by her. So with a nervous hand she selects what she thinks is right (there is a nagging doubt in her mind but she never mentions this) and presses the big red button that starts the process.

Everything seems to be working well and Julie starts to relax. Later that day she hears a commotion in the machine room and the supervisor is shouting at one of the seamstresses who has sewn two left sleeves into a jacket. Julie feels a knot forming in her stomach. Soon every seamstress has done the same thing. Julie has accidentally printed the patterns to cut two left sleeves but no right sleeves. This error causes the company to purchase additional fabric, incur additional cutting time and late delivery of the order. The customer places no further orders for garments. All that waste would have been avoided if someone had coached Julie on her first day in the new job.

Eliminating waste can mean the difference between a huge financial loss and a good profit. To significantly reduce waste in any company you must recognise that there is room for improvement and be willing to take action. Often, as the business owner, you can be 'too close to the forest to see the trees' and spend time fire fighting all your problems as they arise, or you may use the 'this is the way it has always been done' approach, which may have led you to become unsure how to rectify problematic situations. Perhaps you usually solve a current problem using a 'trial and error' method, but this can leave you with no systems in place to recognize and correct similar situations in the future. Unfortunately, most of us do not remember what we did last time and so we reinvent the wheel again.

There is a misconception that waste only comes from mistakes or over-production of unwanted goods. But waste comes from many sources and can be eliminated by diligently finding the causes and implementing ways to prevent it occurring.

Mistakes Waste

Whatever your business, mistakes are costly because they squander time and money. Waste can jeopardize the very existence of your business. Dissatisfied customers take their business elsewhere or are willing to file a law suit against you to recover their losses which result from your company's mistakes. Even if you have adequate insurance cover, if you have been through a lawsuit, it will result in an increase in your insurance rates or, even worse, a cancellation of your insurance policy if you make too many claims. A mistake may not have a negative effect on your customer but your profits can still be negatively affected. Waste costs money.

Mistakes will happen. This chapter is not about absolutely abolishing mistakes, it is about making sure you have done everything in your power to control the mistakes and keep them to the minimum possible level. How do you do this? You put systems into place and ensure that your employees are trained and coached properly, with ample time to learn the skills necessary and in an environment where they know *without question* that they can ask for advice and retraining.

Putting systems in place is not as daunting as it sounds. All it requires is some time and some tests. What do I mean? Well, think of your day-to-day business as a series of small tasks. You do some of the tasks, as do your employees. The quickest way to record and put into place your systems of work, is to record each step involved in each task in sequential order. "Wow," you are thinking, "this will take me weeks!" Delegate!

Firstly, you identify a task and record the individual steps involved to perform it. At the same time note how long it took you to do the task and also to record the process. Once you have your first draft of the steps involved, ask one of your employees to adhere to your recorded steps without deviation and complete that specific piece of work. It is important they follow the steps you have written, in exactly the way you have written them, as this will disclose any errors in your procedure so that you can correct them. Avoid using

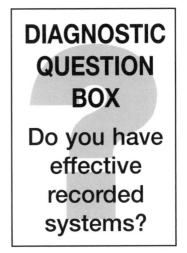

DIAGNOSTIC QUESTION BOX

Do you have effective recorded systems?

one of your more experienced employees as they will automatically perform the task correctly, with or without your exact recorded sequence. It is better to select a novice for this part of the process as they are more likely to follow the sequence without any changes.

Now you know how to perform the task, how long it takes to carry it out and how long it will take to record the steps to execute it. Roughly estimate the number of tasks and the amount of time it will take to record all the processes in your company and use this in your planning. Spend time explaining to your employees the need for the systems and how to record each job they do.

Ask each of your employees to list all the tasks they perform during a business quarter, and also indicate on this list the most appropriate date that each employee believes would be the best time to record each task to ensure minimal disruption to production. This approach involves everyone and it also allows each employee to be responsible for achieving the deadlines, because they have set the deadlines for themselves. Remember to collate all the lists and dates into a schedule to ensure that no two important tasks are being recorded at the same time, if by so doing you would adversely affect production.

Once the tasks have been recorded and tested by another employee and work perfectly, reward each employee (once all the tasks on their list have been completed) with a gift, as they will have saved you money by reducing future mistakes. You now have fully recorded systems which will in future help with staff training and reduce mistakes. Should you ever sell your company or even one of its processes, you will be in a great position to do so. You have saved money and created the possibility to make extra money.

Employee Waste

There are many sections which overlap and involve employees. Here we are going to look specifically at how employees can equal waste. In order to prevent waste when employing staff, you need to be prepared before you recruit. Many small business owners recruit staff because they need an extra pair of hands and because they like or know the person. This is the first major mistake you can make and one of the most costly if all goes wrong, which it often does.

The costs of recruiting and training and employee will vary from job to job and from business to business. Do you know how much it costs you to recruit a new member of staff? The general principle, based on a combination of differing research results, conservatively puts this figure around £3,500 per employee. This means that, if your business employs 100 employees, with an average twenty per cent employee turnover rate, the annual cost would be £70,000. Let's put it another way: if you employ six staff, your recruitment costs per year will be £4,200, before you calculate the salaries.

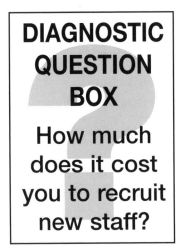

DIAGNOSTIC QUESTION BOX

How much does it cost you to recruit new staff?

$$£3,500 \times 6 = £21,000$$
$$£21,000 \times 20\% = £4,200 \ (6 \times 20\% \times £3,500)$$

I realise that smaller companies can retain staff for longer periods and you will need to do your own calculations. The above formula is only a guideline and is included as a thought-provoking exercise only, because most small business owners do not take the full costs of recruitment into account when looking for new staff, nor do they think about the amount of wasted time and money involved in staff turnover.

What about the less obvious costs of not recruiting and taking too long to fill a vacancy? How much does that cost and where are those hidden costs?

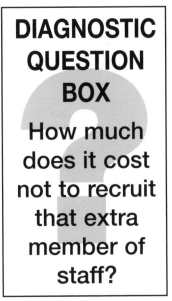

DIAGNOSTIC QUESTION BOX

How much does it cost not to recruit that extra member of staff?

Remaining staff

You need to consider the impact that an unfilled vacancy could have on the remaining staff in terms of morale, productivity and mistakes under pressure. These can cause the remaining staff to consider looking elsewhere for work, which means you may end up with even more vacancies to fill.

Experienced staff

Remember that an experienced, trained member of staff will take with them, when they leave, knowledge about your company, details of your customer base, your procedures and other very valuable information and skills which a competitor may be happy to acquire.

Lost customers

You also need to consider any lost customers as the result of an understaffed department or company. Even a back office job can have an adverse effect on the service or product, which could result in your customers going elsewhere. Often, the customer will not tell you why they are not doing business with you any more; they just quietly disappear.

Dissatisfied customers

A dissatisfied customer will tell as many as ten or twelve other people (potential customers or current customers) about the poor service or product they received from your company. There is nothing you can do about this because, usually, you do not know it is happening.

Market position

Any of these situations could lead to the ultimate waste – the loss of your hard-earned market share to your competitors.

Investment

Consider hiring staff as an investment in your future and that of your company rather than a liability and a cost. How could your company grow, change and become more effective with the right people? What new products and services could you offer?

Outsourcing

If you have no time to find new staff, consider outsourcing. Hire an employment agency to find the extra member of staff. The cost of outsourcing sometimes puts small companies off using their services. So before you go ahead and outsource, work out how much it will actually cost you in time spent, using the formula in Chapter 3, Time Is Money, under the section 'How to cost time'.

When you know the hourly cost of your time you can calculate how long it takes to write the advertisement, filter the applications, interview the applicants, and request and read the references. Only when you have gone through this process will you really know the costs involved and decide whether to deal with the recruitment process yourself or outsource. Remember, if you do not need a full-time employee you can hire a consultant or temporary member of staff to fill the gap, and it is quite common for a temporary member of staff to accept invitations to become a permanent employee.

Always evaluate all the risks and all the benefits (in monetary terms) associated with your decision to recruit or not to recruit. The decision could become a costly mistake which may impact your bottom line for years to come.

Time Waste

Time management was covered in Chapter 3; this section deals with employee time wasting. There are four overt ways of employees not utilising their time effectively: use of the internet, personal telephone calls, general chatting, and travelling between locations.

Internet

The internet can be a boom or a bust technology for small companies. Your staff may need to surf the web for many reasons and they may only be surfing for information to help the growth of your company. Here is the rub – surfing the net usually takes three times longer than anticipated and surfing without very tight timescales and clearly defined outcomes is a waste of time.

One way to control the time allotted to surfing is to furnish all internet staff with alarm clocks, giving them restricted surfing time slots, asking them to use this process for a month and record the results. Allocate time in minutes to surf the net and set the alarm. As soon as the alarm goes off they must stop searching, and mark their results on a scale of 1 to 10 (10 being fully effective and all necessary information found). At the end of the month discuss with them their thoughts and feelings about surfing the net and decide together the best way forward based on the outcome of the discussion.

E-mails are another potential time waster. You may need to establish a written procedure to give your employees clarity and direction on the sending of e-mails for personal use. Some companies exert strict control over personal e-mails during working hours, which can result in disciplinary action for employees who break the rules.

Telephone calls

Most employees use your telephones occasionally for personal calls and it is up to you to set and keep the guidelines for their usage. Also it is worth noting that a good salesperson will build a strong and effective rapport with customers and this type of telephone call could sound like a personal call. While setting guidelines for company telephone usage you might

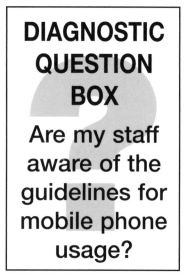

DIAGNOSTIC QUESTION BOX

Are my staff aware of the guidelines for mobile phone usage?

also consider curbing the use of personal mobile phones during work time for calls and text messages. Both of these activities can devour company time and therefore company money.

Chatting

General chatting can be a real boost for the company and for the morale of employees, but only if guidelines are established and the customer or work always comes first. Another consideration is gossiping and backbiting. Sometimes employees overstep the boundaries and this causes loss of energy, motivation and company time.

You need to keep a tight rein and clear framework for chatting and a careful ear for the grey border between chat and gossip, as one can so easily slip into the other. A good general rule is everything said about everyone in the company should be acceptable to the person spoken about and should be repeatable to that person. This also includes what you say, so you should set the example.

Travelling

The other area of wastage, in time and money, is travel costs. It is advisable for you or your office manager to have already been on all the journeys that you expect your employees to take and to set tables for expenses. You need to allow for the exceptional circumstance, for example, the motorway being closed or flights being cancelled. Watch out for employees who are consistently outside of the travel tables and address suspected abuse immediately, as precedents are quick to make and hard to change. If everyone who travels has a copy of the travel table and is clear of your expectations about their expenses, you will have less aggravation and more appropriate expenses.

Stationery/Product Waste

There will always be some wastage with regards to stationery. Employees will often assume they can 'borrow' things like pens, sticky pads and paper. If this is kept within normal acceptable (acceptable to you) boundaries, some business owners use the 'blind eye' technique when weighing the borrowing against the loss of morale and motivation if the employee is challenged. Waste in the stationery cupboard can also take the form of ordering too much and therefore some of your cash flow is stockpiled in the stationery cupboard.

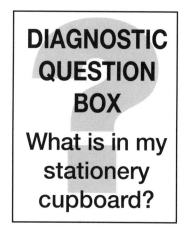

DIAGNOSTIC QUESTION BOX

What is in my stationery cupboard?

Order stationery on a just-in-time system. This also applies to any and all products supplied to you. This system means exactly what it says; you set up a process with a reminding facility which alerts you or your employees when you are just about to use the last available item and with sufficient time to order and receive replacements. Keep an eye on photocopier use and abuse.

Opportunity Waste

Every company has missed opportunities in one way or another, either in sales, advertising, point of sales, recruiting, strategic alliances, not licensing ideas or processes, training staff who leave, buying stock at premium rates instead of planning for the sales seasons – and I am sure you can think of many more. One of the commonest examples of opportunity waste is failing to follow up on enquiries from potential customers.

Spend time looking at your company to spot the opportunities that you could exploit. If you cannot find any then put an incentive scheme together with a good reward for any member of staff who identifies an opportunity you do not currently have and which increases your revenue or reduces waste.

Energy Waste

Consider areas where you could be wasting energy. Replace light bulbs and strip lighting with low voltage, long-life equivalents. Ensure that lights are switched off when not needed. Check what happens when the cleaners are working. Are all the lights in the building on during the cleaning process or are they working floor by floor, turning off the lights as they go? Heating and air-conditioning should have time and thermostatic controls fitted, and equipment should not be left on stand-by. Encourage your staff to be energy conscious. Check your energy bills regularly for early warning signs of upward trends. Keep informed of the market pricing structures and change suppliers if you see a cost saving. Make sure all your equipment is serviced regularly as poorly serviced equipment can use significantly more energy than properly serviced ones.

Cleaning Waste

Money is often wasted in cleaning the premises of a company. Whether you hire your own cleaning staff or if you outsource the cleaning contract, usually there are areas to save money. If you hire your own cleaning staff check the contract and see if you are paying by the hour or job. If you are paying by the hour, do random checks to see if the cleaners are on your premises when they are supposed to be. Are you paying for the cleaning products and, if so, is there a more cost-effective way of purchasing them or using cheaper alternatives?

Outsourcing the cleaning contract can be helpful in controlling costs. You will generally pay more for outsourced cleaning and you need to be very clear on which option is best for you. For a more accurate picture, remember to include in the equation the amount of time you spend on organising your cleaning arrangements.

Consider strategic alliances with relation to cleaning. What are the companies in your building or close proximity to you doing about cleaning? Can you share a cleaner or even a cleaning contract and spread the costs between companies? If you can organise a group of companies you will be in a stronger negotiating position with the cleaning contractor and you could save yourself a good percentage of your cleaning costs. If you cannot arrange to combine the cleaners, perhaps you could combine your cleaning product purchases and therefore increase your negotiating power to reduce those costs.

You must be fully committed to eliminating all areas of waste, large and small. Develop good waste management systems that will eliminate wastage, reduce your costs and increase your profits. Perhaps the saying should be: 'Where there's waste there's money!'

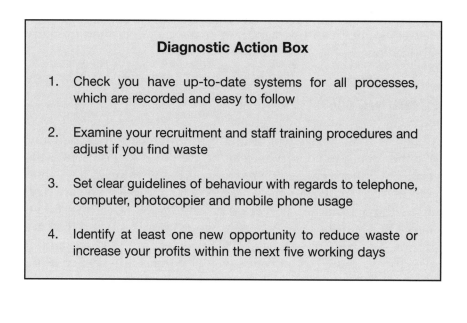

Diagnostic Action Box

1. Check you have up-to-date systems for all processes, which are recorded and easy to follow

2. Examine your recruitment and staff training procedures and adjust if you find waste

3. Set clear guidelines of behaviour with regards to telephone, computer, photocopier and mobile phone usage

4. Identify at least one new opportunity to reduce waste or increase your profits within the next five working days

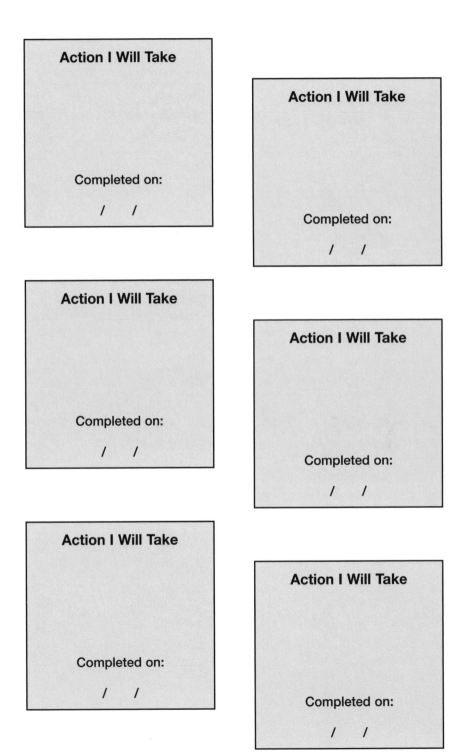

Action I Will Take

Completed on:

/   /

Action I Will Take

Completed on:

/   /

Action I Will Take

Completed on:

/   /

Action I Will Take

Completed on:

/   /

Action I Will Take

Completed on:

/   /

Action I Will Take

Completed on:

/   /

Chapter Fifteen

Intellectual Money

Generate money from your intellectual assets and any
intellectual property which you may not know you already have.
Protect those assets. All company directors should read this chapter.
Companies that have the potential to grow from research and
development will particularly benefit.

Synopsis

You will have heard of copyright and trade marks before. This
chapter is about much more. It includes intellectual assets and
intellectual property. Some of the ideas and ways you can capitalise on what you already have or know could surprise you.

Intellectual assets in the form of recordable knowledge may
have a market value. Intellectual property rights are parts of your
business which are legally protected by statute law. They have
the potential to produce an extra income stream and you may
already have them in your company.

Jeff Sacree loved surfing and started a company making custom
surfboards for local surfers and retail shops in Devon and Cornwall.

Surfing in the chilly waters off the Cornish coasts can give surfers
an 'ice-cream headache' especially during the winter months. The
term 'ice-cream headache' refers to a phenomenon of surfing in
cold water and its effect on the surfer's head, which has been compared to how it might feel if it were put into a vice with pressure
applied to the temples on a gradually increasing basis. This painful
condition is at its worst when cold water surfing in North
Cornwall's winter seas.

The condition of ice-cream headache could range from mildly bothersome to acutely painful and debilitating. Because this condition would affect the surfers' performance and enjoyment of the sport, Jeff decided that something had to be done. So he invested time and effort into solving the problem by designing a lightweight heat retaining helmet for himself to prevent the distractions of ice-cream headaches when he surfed.

Other local surfers became interested in the helmet and it started to sell in small numbers. Jeff got wind that the Royal National Lifeboat Institute was looking to replace helmets currently worn by lifeboat crews as the ones they were using were thought to be unsafe.

Jeff offered his solution and services and eventually, after several years of hard work, research and development, the MK5 Marine Safety helmet became the first marine safety standard in Europe, and created a benchmark for others to follow. This enabled Jeff's business, Gecko Headgear, to expand and take on additional production staff. The helmet offered a solution but was by no means perfect, so research and development continued.

Over the following years various models were tried and tested to overcome the problem of designing a one-size lightweight shell that would offer good head protection. Eventually, after the culmination of eight years' research and development, a design was developed which set the standard and was, at that time, the only design-approved marine safety helmet available.

Then Jeff became aware of a cheap imported copy helmet which was flooding the market. At this time Jeff's helmet was not a registered design. This caused some concern until Jeff heard that a design can be covered by the Design Right Law without being a registered design. He hired the services of a specialist and won his case, which eventually restricted the sales of copy helmets.

His company has gone from strength to strength and now has several styles of helmets, including one which features a patented inflatable liner. This advance in the evolution of the Gecko Marine Safety Helmet has been incorporated into several hybrid versions now made by Jeff's company.

This story has been printed by kind permission of Jeff Sacree. You can visit Jeff's website www.geckoheadgear.com to find out more about the amazing 'ice-cream headache' helmet.

In today's information age, what you know is more important than what you do or produce. It is because of this new era that I have written this chapter, and I encourage you to take time to consider the points raised in the light of your own company's activities and assets. There are two main areas where income can be generated or protected: intellectual assets and intellectual property and you may already have them. Both of these areas have the potential to produce extra income.

Intellectual Property Rights

Intellectual property rights, listed below, are the parts of a business which are legally protected by statute law and need maximising and managing to realise income or protect income generation. In the current knowledge-based economy, these rights are becoming especially important to businesses and individuals. Intellectual property rights cover a number of different legal aspects, with different rules to protect commercial ideas and technology.

The list is not definitive and all the information in this chapter is offered with the implicit understanding that you will seek specialist legal advice where your business or personal information is concerned.

Confidentiality agreements

These agreements are often written where specialist knowledge or systems are being used or created and usually have specific binding words relating to non-disclosure. There are two concerns with these agreements:

1. They are only as good as the intention of the person who signs them. So if unscrupulous people are after your intellectual property, they will sign them anyway believing they are unlikely to be sued for any breach of contract.

2. Many businesses (business-to-business ventures) will refuse to sign them.

You must have any contracts concerning confidentially drawn up by a lawyer and be prepared to take action if agreements are broken, and you can prove it.

A contract can also be useful as a possible preventive measure to inhibit or dissuade an employee who is tempted to take your client base and either start up in business for themselves or offer it to your competitors. A contract will not stop resolute thieves because they may already know that litigation is expensive and time consuming. Most employers are not willing to go that far.

Copyright ©

This is a right against copying (this book, for example) and not against prior, subsequent or simultaneous origination and it lasts for seventy years after the death of the originator. It covers the following:

- Technical drawings
  Technical reports
  Training manuals
  Industrial manuals
  Technical manuals
  Databases, etc.

- Books
  Plays
  Drawings
  Photographs
  Paintings
  Sculptures
  Music, songs
  Videos, broadcasts
  Films, etc.

- Computer software
  Computer images
  Computer manuals, etc.

DIAGNOSTIC QUESTION BOX

Is there a manual or written process you should copyright?

This law is notably difficult to enforce as you need to prove the chain of copying. It has been known for software writers to add an intentional spelling mistake, so the person who copies will not notice when photocopying the materials, but the copying can be linked back to the originator.

Design right

Design right prevents deliberate copying of the appearance or form of things and can be important with regard to your company's branding. The opening story highlighted an area which many people do not consider when thinking about their business. This right covers three-dimensional copyright such as original shapes and objects. The design right also covers internal configurations and semi-conductor chips. It lasts for ten years with a right to license after five years, and includes texture or materials, contours, lines, colours, shape and its ornamentation.

Registered design ®

This is different from design right due to the fact that it must be registered. There is a 'year of grace' after the product has entered the market which means you can launch the product and, if you decide to make some small alterations because of feedback received, you can make the changes and register the final version.

The positive side of this is the 'year of grace'; the downside is that during the first twelve months the product is at risk. This is a decision that you and your directors alone can make. I recommend that if you are going to register a design you employ the services of an expert in the field at the beginning, rather than use the do-it-yourself approach.

Registration lasts for twenty-five years (from the first registration) and has been harmonised throughout Europe. A wide range of designs can be registered including graphic symbols, packaging and parts of complex products. It is considered by some experts that using a registered design may be easier and cheaper than registering trade marks.

Registered trade marks™

Trade marks can include signs, sounds, smells and touch, but although this seems wide ranging, there are many restrictions. A trade mark lasts indefinitely provided it is renewed after ten years. Do a global trade mark search prior to starting out on registration. Be aware of 'grandfather's rights', which can apply if the mark has been in the public domain for eight years. The registration process can be costly and a lengthy process.

Patents

An easy way to think about a patent is as a bargain between you, the inventor, and the state, where there is full disclosure to the state. The invention must be capable of being manufactured, novel, not a discovery or an idea and not of great security danger or value to the state. It lasts for twenty years from the date of the first filing. It has sometimes been considered better to keep all the secrets rather than share them with the state. I recommend that you use a patent agency specialist if you decide to take this route. Contact the Chartered Institute of Patent Agents for more information.

Worldwide rights

You need to do due diligence with regards to your rights around the world. Whilst you might be covered in Europe you may not be covered elsewhere. Before exporting you should find out how to protect your ideas in your target markets. If your product has international appeal you may decide to apply for protection worldwide prior to launching.

Remember, a right will only be as good as your ability to enforce it. Consider exactly what you want to reveal, have an intellectual property right strategy and hire an expert to audit and assist with the applications. It will save time in the long run.

Licensing

One alternative to working alone is to offer a licence (for use) to a market leader or a medium-sized company. The advantage of the medium-sized company over the market leader is they will need you as much as you need them, and they probably will not tie you up for months or years in red tape.

A medium-sized company could be looking for a growth idea to take them to the next business level and may not have the expertise within their own company. It is important to have confidentiality agreements signed before you reveal your ideas.

Another alternative is to form a strategic alliance with a couple of other companies who have complementary skills and interests. To reduce potential conflict and misunderstandings, which could arise when different companies are trying to work together, you could set up a separate limited company solely to produce a prototype and generate interest in investment from outside the alliance. A tip, should you go this route, is to have a neutral figurehead for the newly created company in the form of a non-executive chairperson, as this will help ensure speedy resolution if conflicts arise. Remember you will need to like the people involved.

It is important to employ the services of a specialist. The Institute of International Licensing Practitioners is a good place to start. You will need to consider the parties involved, what is being licensed, how long the licence should last, what type of licence, the calculation of the fees payable or royalties, the location and scope of the licence and any caveats you wish to include. Other areas needing attention include who has ownership, where should the payments go, what and who is responsible for quality control, and what happens in the event of non-performance of any of the clauses of the licence.

DIAGNOSTIC QUESTION BOX

Who do I know would make a good strategic partner?

When working with such partners you will need to have a working prototype or model, proof of your market research and estimated production costing. Also, your cost-to-price ratios will be required at this stage. As a very rough guideline, three-and-a-half to four times the cost of production could be used. Therefore, if it costs £2 to make, the price to sell could be between £7 to £8 pounds. If there are similar products on the market already, your market research will provide you with a very good gauge as to your product viability.

A licence can give you and your vendors ways of generating an income, such as an annual fee or a percentage of sales, and is worth considering when looking for ways to capitalise on your assets.

Intellectual Assets/Intangible Assets

By intellectual assets I am referring to intangible things which can be coded or written down and sold into a market, or assets with market value, including any human capital. For example, when delegates attend my business coach training courses or life coach training courses they come for the information and also for the 'Curly Experience'. Intangible assets, such as the value of people, are often referred to as intellectual capital.

Some of the things to consider as intellectual assets or capital

- Contracts
- Customer information
- Specialist know-how or know-how-not-to
- Supplier knowledge
- Customers who enhance company profile
- Branding
- Goodwill
- Reputation (author/speaker, etc.)
- Accreditations
- By royal appointment
- Process procedures

- Trade secrets
- Domain names
- Company name

The importance of intellectual assets is often overlooked by businesses because of the intangibility of the asset. However, you could find that a key employee leaves your company with strategic and specific information or know-how which has not been recorded anywhere. This could leave your company exposed to greater competition or halted production time and even reduce your company's value.

When you are working with strategic partners, universities, contractors, board members or anyone who could possibly consider they have contributed to the design or development of your product, ensure that all parties involved have signed your contract and are aware that all the rights are assigned to your company. This also applies to any of your suppliers (printers, image consultants, public relations, marketing gurus, website designers, et al.) who would be under commission for brochures, leaflets, software, logos, branding or any work which you consider yours by right.

Another area to mention is your employees. Contracts of employment should cover intellectual property, intellectual assets and confidentiality to reduce your exposure. You need to make sure that your employees fully understand the value of your intellectual assets and that you expect confidentiality in all matters relating to your company. Make sure they are fully aware that confidentiality includes casual discussions in the pub or with friends, as it has been known for ideas to appear on the market by competitors because of overheard conversations.

There could be further sources of income from your intellectual assets in the form of licensing, franchising

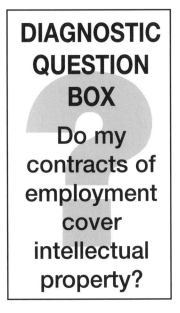

DIAGNOSTIC QUESTION BOX

Do my contracts of employment cover intellectual property?

or short-term contracting. Ask yourself this question: "Am I managing my intellectual assets for the maximum gain?" and then take appropriate action.

In the current knowledge-based economy, intellectual property rights and intellectual assets are important to businesses and individuals, and it is up to you to manage these resources to maximum effect.

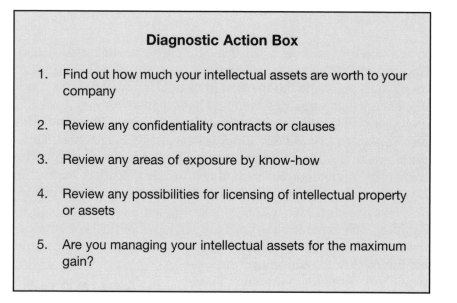

Diagnostic Action Box

1. Find out how much your intellectual assets are worth to your company

2. Review any confidentiality contracts or clauses

3. Review any areas of exposure by know-how

4. Review any possibilities for licensing of intellectual property or assets

5. Are you managing your intellectual assets for the maximum gain?

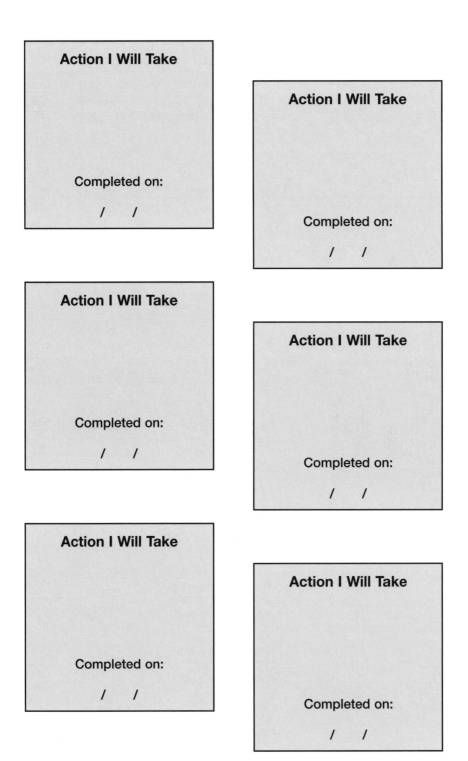

Action I Will Take

Completed on:

/   /

Action I Will Take

Completed on:

/   /

Action I Will Take

Completed on:

/   /

Action I Will Take

Completed on:

/   /

Action I Will Take

Completed on:

/   /

Action I Will Take

Completed on:

/   /

Chapter Sixteen

Outsourcing

They say a problem shared is a problem halved, and outsourcing can better those odds if planned and managed well

Synopsis

This chapter looks at the popular alternative to taking on extra staff. It covers the benefits and disadvantages of outsourcing, along with the hows, whys and wherefores of the process; invitations to tender, TUPE restrictions, implementation and management. It also looks at ways to make outsourcing happen as a smooth process rather than becoming an extra burden.

Susan White was the owner of a recruitment company in Bristol, and she leased a one-room office with a small kitchenette and separate toilet. She had always cleaned the unit herself until her business started to grow. The demand on her time to run the business forced her to look at areas to save time and, naturally, she decided to find a cleaner. A simple task she thought.

Whilst collecting her mail she discussed this with one of the other tenants in the building and discovered that a contractor was cleaning most of the other units. She called the company and the manager assured her that he knew exactly what she wanted and would send her the same agreement as the other tenants, which she signed.

During the first month of employing the cleaning company she realised that the things she thought would be cleaned were not being done, so she decided to have a word with the manager. She explained that the rubbish bin was not being emptied, and some days her desk was cleaned and other days it was not, the cups in the kitchen were not washed or put away, the carpet had not been vacuumed, the toilet had not been cleaned nor had the toilet roll been changed.

The manager sighed and explained that she had signed the contract which clearly stated the following:

- Rubbish bins will only be emptied if a bin liner has been used

- Desks need to be cleared

- Cleaners would switch the dishwashers on but were not responsible for loading the washer or for individual item washing (which means they do not wash dishes)

- The carpet will only be cleaned if the owner provides the vacuum cleaner

- The toilet was not included in the contract and would need higher rates because it was considered a hazardous area

Susan was amazed and angry. She slammed down the phone and pulled her copy of the contract out of the file and read the small print. It was there in black and white – the manager was right! She had not spent time writing down exactly what actions she took when she cleaned each night, each week and monthly. She also assumed her situation would be the same as the other tenants and she would therefore be happy with the same service. So now she was paying for a partial clean and still needed to spend her own time cleaning.

Outsourcing or Business Process Outsourcing (BPO) is rapidly becoming an effective alternative, and companies of all sizes are using this for competitive advantage. Outsourcing provides the opportunity for large or small companies to have various business or support processes undertaken by outside providers who offer cheaper, faster or better specialist services. The main benefits – cost and competition – seem obvious. Another consideration when looking into outsourcing is that it enables companies to focus more on their core business. Outsourcing non-essential functions frees up time and the resources of a company, allowing all concerned to give attention to what they do best. Usually, small companies find renewed motivation and creativity for their core business once they have released themselves from mundane activities.

Interestingly, many small companies or sole traders already out-source without acknowledging it. Such functions include book-keeping, accounting, payroll, technical support and web hosting. These are functions which usually require specialist expertise, and the small business owner is happy to outsource these tasks and rarely sees them as outsourcing. However, there are more and more services available, such as answering services, customer care, call centres and even manufacturing, which offer all compa-nies the opportunity to recover time and resources, thus enabling them to focus on what they are good at.

I realised very quickly that I did not have the time to answer the telephone and that I could not answer it when I was out of the office. I did not want to risk prospective clients not leaving a mes-sage because they thought I could not handle their business. At the time, I had insufficient funds and time to employ someone just to answer my telephone. Instead, I employed the services of a tele-phone answering company. This was one of the first tasks I out-sourced and it proved to be a huge success. I even had one customer who said, "I chose your company because the other providers I contacted had answering machines or mobile phones and I did not trust them."

What can be Outsourced?

- Telephone answering
- Customer service
- Sales
- Public relations and marketing
- All information technology processes
- Office tasks – typing, photo-copying, data entry, etc.
- Transport
- Accounting
- Payroll
- Manufacturing

DIAGNOSTIC QUESTION BOX

What process could you outsource, and if you did, what would you gain?

If there is a process, there usually is a company offering that service for a price.

What to Consider

When you decide that you need to outsource there are several things to take into consideration before, during and after you have outsourced.

Finance

This includes the costs involved and the savings you may make in real terms. Savings are made not only on recruitment, salary, benefits in kind, pensions, National Insurance and tax relating to employees, but also on saved time. Once you know the amount of time saved you can work out the savings in monetary terms, by using the formula in Chapter 3, Time is Money, under the heading 'How to cost time'. Remember to include the cost of time needed to research, define and select the service provider, as well as the ongoing management of the outsourcing project. Also, figure into your calculations your staff turnover as this might relieve the costs and help with the decision process.

Specific details of the service expected

This will need to be outlined, tested and measured with a pilot run-through to ensure there are no deletions or additions. Take the simple example of Susan at the beginning of this chapter. Had she outlined specifically what she did daily, weekly and monthly before she outsourced her cleaning, her life would have been a lot easier.

Staff affected by the outsourcing

If you have staff it is very important that each of their roles has a detailed job description and any key performance indicators related to the role. See Chapter 11, Staff Strategies, for more details on how this is achieved. There are three options affecting your staff during the outsourcing process: transfer to the outsourcing supplier, redeployment within your company or redundancy (either compulsory or voluntary). Remember too, that staff may see outsourcing as a threat to their own job security, so keep them in the picture.

Should you decide to transfer your staff to the outsource provider, you will need to ensure the transfers are completed under the terms of the Transfer of Undertakings (Protection of Employment) Regulations 1981, more commonly known as TUPE. You will need a copy of the Department of Trade and Industry (DTI) leaflet, PL699 – REV4 Employment Rights on the Transfer of an Undertaking. Part of the regulations state: *"Thus employees' continuity of employment is preserved, as are their terms and conditions of employment under their contracts of employment (except for certain occupational pension rights)."* Visit the website for further details at www.dti.gov.uk

Redundancy can be voluntary or compulsory, but one thing to keep in mind is that you cannot make an employee redundant if their job continues to exist. A job is considered to continue to exist when transferred to another employer, as in outsourcing. Think of it like this: jobs become redundant before the staff do.

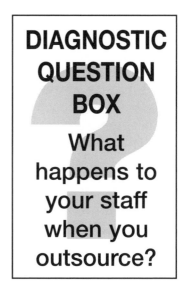

DIAGNOSTIC QUESTION BOX
What happens to your staff when you outsource?

Staff considerations in outsourcing projects can be a minefield, not only with the impact on motivation but mainly regarding the legislation. I recommend you spend time and energy on due diligence, and I also recommend you hire the services of an employment law expert. When communicating with staff, make sure you announce only when you are completely ready, do not make promises you cannot keep and ensure everything said or written is clear and accurate. This will reduce the problems caused by the gossip grapevine and the motivation dip which often occurs with outsourcing.

Current assets

These need to be considered. If you have equipment related to the outsourcing you will need to take the following into consideration:

1. Are you going to transfer the asset to the supplier?
2. Are you going sell the asset on the open market?
3. Are you going keep the asset?
4. Is the asset under guarantee or does it have a service agreement?
5. Is the asset under a leasing agreement?
6. What is the book value of the asset?
7. What happens to the asset at the end of the outsourcing contract?

Spend time planning the best way to deal with the asset. Think of ways which do not have a cost implication and which are easy to implement.

Invitation to tender (ITT)

This is the best approach to outsourcing. Sometimes you can be lured into the trap that just because your friend uses ABC, they must be good enough for you. Remember Susan White's story at the beginning of this chapter. I am not saying that you will not use your friend's supplier; but I am saying that you should know what service you want and get several companies to apply for the contract. This makes the process more formal and sets the tone for working together with a supplier. There are many books on the subject, but to whet your appetite, here is a brief outline. There are six main areas to cover when putting together your ITT:

1. A brief introduction that contains the practical process of the tender and the contents, along with page numbering; a description of your company, possibly your company's annual report and what you want to outsource; supplier deadlines and penalties for failure to respond in your requested format; confidentiality clauses; the scope and the nature of the service required; and – the often forgotten – what is not required.

2. Supplier instructions including the timetable, the format they have to respond in, the evaluation process and any contractual and reference site details.

3. A complete detailed requirement overview which includes the description of the service you are looking to outsource (this is where the staffing and asset transfers are mentioned), authority for your company to manage the project and any special requirements you have.

4. Supplier information should include what you want to know about the supplier, such as their background, expertise, qualifications/accreditations, references you can follow up, reference sites (companies who already use the supplier's services and are willing to allow you to visit), how they propose to provide the service and any exit strategies or penalties for the ending of the contract.

5. Terms and conditions for working together. Information needed here could be the quotation valid dates, prices, discounts, penalties and any additional charges. Take the example of Susan White – will you or the supplier provide the cleaning materials?

6. Any other information you require or wish to provide.

Once you have prepared your ITT you will need to offer it out to tender. This might involve placing an advertisement/announcement in the local press or specialist trade publications inviting potential suppliers to express an interest in tendering for the contract. The advertisement should include the closing date for the tenders to arrive. It is normal during this stage for suppliers to contact you for further information on the contract.

Now you need to decide on the suppliers by selecting a shortlist of preferred tenders. You should, at this stage in the process, take up references, visit reference sites, investigate the financial stability of the suppliers, examine compliance documentation and execute due diligence to make certain the supplier you finally select will satisfy all your criteria. The final selection can be made by placing the shortlist of candidates on a selection criteria matrix which gives marks to each supplier based on single decisive factors which are totalled. On the opposite page is an incomplete model of the type of matrix I am describing to give you some ideas for getting started.

DIAGNOSTIC QUESTION BOX

How are you going to choose the right supplier for your business?

In the left column write all the criteria you wish to use to select a supplier (some ideas are already in the matrix.) Along the top of the list put the names of the shortlisted suppliers. Measure each criterion against each provider on a scale of 1 to 10, using 1 to mean not provided and a sliding scale of provision up to 10 indicating fully meeting your criteria and your personal requirements. You can also add weighting if a criteria is very important.

Once you have decided on your criteria, designed your matrix and completed the totals, you should be in a better position to make your choice of supplier. At this stage you will need yet more due diligence, as the contracts will be drawn up along with a service level agreement.

A service level agreement specifies how each part of the service will be provided, to exactly what standard it will be provided, and when it will be provided and when it will not be provided. The agreement should also contain the measures by which the service will be deemed as complying with the contract and what should be done in the event the service does not match the service level agreed. I strongly advise involving a solicitor at this stage (or earlier).

In contracts where you are outsourcing a specialist service, employ an expert or specialist solicitor or lawyer. Specialists will be more accustomed to dealing with any contract areas of contention, special terminology and contractual abnormalities required to protect you.

	Provider			
Criteria	Achievement Specialists Ltd	Supplier B	Supplier C	Supplier D
Compliance with ITT				
Accreditation/qualification				
Affordability				
References				
Professional indemnity and public liability insurance				
Financial check				
Experienced staff				
References				
Reference site visit				
Dedicated account contact				
Negative points				
Totals				

See this cost as an investment; it is always better to walk away from a contract at this stage than to find yourself embroiled in litigation later. My reasoning for this is not just based on the costs of contractual litigation but also on the time you will spend preparing the documentation, attending hearings and worrying about it. If you need any further persuasion, calculate the cost of your time by the hour and multiply it by thousands, or ask someone who has been down the litigation route.

Implementation and continual management

This is the final stage of the outsourcing process. There will always be a transitional period when the service is handed over to the supplier and this needs careful management and control. You should have included the authority to manage the project in the ITT and, therefore, when the inevitable disagreements arise you will be in a good position to handle them. Remember you can refer back to the service level agreement when necessary and also remember that staff old and new may be unsure of their roles. Diplomacy is paramount during the whole process, to establish and maintain good working relationships with staff and suppliers.

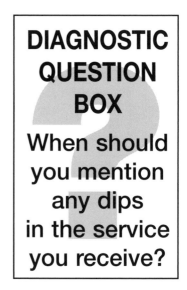

DIAGNOSTIC QUESTION BOX

When should you mention any dips in the service you receive?

Measurement is part of the management remit when outsourcing and you will need to measure your customer satisfaction, performance against service level, ongoing costs and productivity. At the start of the outsourcing project you will probably be measuring on a daily basis and, as the outsourcing settles down to the level of service you are looking for on a regular basis, you will extend the measuring periods. The key is to measure on a regular and consistent basis.

End of contract strategies

End of contract strategies are very important to consider before you start the outsourcing project and should be included in the ITT. Often the exit is the reverse of the process. You will need to decide the main objectives of the exit, who will be responsible for what, who owns what (including any copyrights and assets) between your company and the supplier. If any of the employees were transferred (TUPE) staff, hopefully you will have made contingencies for this in the contract. However, I recommend you get professional advice prior to the end of contract regarding staff.

DIAGNOSTIC QUESTION BOX

What do you need to do to prepare for the end of a contract?

A couple of tips

If there are any changes to the service, no matter how large or small, treat them formally and document them. If you allow any changes to the service level agreement without notifying the supplier formally, it could cause problems at any stage of the contract. Always negotiate with your supplier if problems arise.

If you have documented all deviations from the agreement you are in a strong position to negotiate and this is usually cheaper than litigation. Remember, if you have employees, managing the relationships during the times of change created by outsourcing is a task which you must be ready to take on.

Outsourcing is a way of making real cost reductions for your business and your customers alike. It also offers an opportunity to expand your product or service range and increase your competitive advantage.

You need to decide if the costs and considerations mentioned in this chapter are worth the benefits, and if the answer is yes, then plan carefully before you go ahead. Good luck.

Diagnostic Action Box

1. If you do not already have all your tasks/processes recorded – do it now!

2. How much does each task/process cost to perform?

3. How would it save time and money if you outsourced specific tasks or processes?

4. Are the tasks/processes you already have outsourced (e.g. cleaning) performing to expected service levels? Do you need to review them?

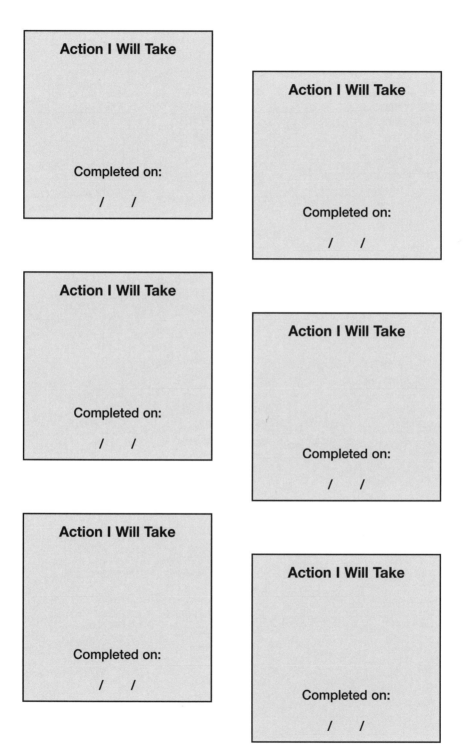

Action I Will Take

Completed on:

/   /

Action I Will Take

Completed on:

/   /

Action I Will Take

Completed on:

/   /

Action I Will Take

Completed on:

/   /

Action I Will Take

Completed on:

/   /

Action I Will Take

Completed on:

/   /

Chapter Seventeen

Succession Planning

The time will come when you want to retire and enjoy the benefits of having owned your business or practice. The time to start planning for this is now.

Synopsis

When the founder or owner moves on, some businesses continue in good health and even grow under enthusiastic and innovative new ownership. Others grow out of all recognition in different arenas and, alas, a similar number simply fold and disappear forever. This chapter outlines some considerations that will help to ensure that you protect your interests when you decide it is time for you, your business or practice to effectively 'divorce' from each other.

When the garage and workshop originally opened on a World War II bomb site in 1946, it was a car dealership. Because it fitted in well with its rural surroundings by the local branch line railway station, the council even approved the installation of underground petrol storage tanks to feed the single, hand-operated, forecourt pump, along with a designated stand for George Jones's cherished pre-war taxi.

The branch line closed and the station was converted into a house. Over the next few years a succession of property developers used this as a precedent for building over the adjoining sidings. The garage stopped car sales but the workshop continued to undertake repairs. That was several years ago. George continued to enjoy a healthy business and even welcomed the housing developments because they brought new trade. Eventually the houses had taken over the nearby fields and then, despite newly introduced planning zones, a supermarket and filling station arrived. George could not compete on price so he mothballed his old petrol pump as a bit of local history and featured it as a logo for his 'repair shop only' business.

This year, when so many modern cars had computerised engine management systems and sophisticated electronics, he decided that enough was enough. His children were not in the least interested in running the business and, as a garage, it no longer had any significant market value. As he signed the sale documents to a developer with plans to build flats on the site, he thought, "If only I had sold up 15 years ago, I would have got a good price for the site, premises, tools and goodwill." Instead, he was about to accept a sum that bore no relationship at all to his years of experience and tender loving care. It was less than a third of the going concern value of all those years before.

Before the garage was demolished, George discovered a long-lost vestige of entrepreneurial flair and had the foresight to take several coloured photographs. These were regularly sold for use in advertising campaigns, illustrations in 'yesteryear' magazines and books, and even as postcards in the supermarket. He has enlargements of the original photographs on the wall of his lounge. Many evenings his glance falls across them as he heaves a deep sigh and thinks, yet again, "If only ..."

At a business seminar I attended several years ago the keynote speaker began his presentation by asking what we thought was the most important thing to consider when starting a business. He wrote all the suggestions on a flip chart. Then he took a red pen and scrawled 'No!' right across them all. When he announced that the first thing we should all have was a 'get-out plan', there was a stunned silence, broken by a few laughs from those who thought he was joking. But he was absolutely serious.

Without wishing to depress you, it has been said that there are only three absolute certainties in life. These are birth, death and taxes. The same applies to your business venture. The big difference is that you can control and plan for its virtual death, just as you did for its birth, and to minimise your tax bills. By virtual death I simply mean that the original founder (you) decides to dispose of the business for whatever reason.

Enough talk of death; let us consider the more positive issue of vibrant health. Generally, the healthier your business, the more reward you will get when you sell it. If you are planning to pass it on to someone in your family, they will have a more valuable asset. After all, nobody will thank you for selling (or giving them) a sickly, failing business.

DIAGNOSTIC QUESTION BOX

Have you written your get-out plan yet?

Even gifts and inheritances attract punitive taxes and, if you sell your business, you may be liable for capital gains tax. (Your offspring could even be in line to pay death duties and inheritance tax.) When preparing your 'get-out plan' your first step must be to consult a solicitor, an accountant and a qualified financial adviser. Go along with some specific questions to ask and, if you are not happy with the answers, seek a second or third independent opinion. Your prime objective is to gain maximum benefit whilst reducing your potential tax liabilities to an absolute minimum. And because the laws concerning such matters tend to change frequently, as will your circumstances, you need to review your plans every year. This way you will stay ahead of the game, maintain control and keep all your options open for the best succession method and timing.

If selling up is your preferred 'get-out' route, remember that most selling prices are closely related to turnover, profit and the value of tangible assets. All businesses have regularly repeating cycles of peaks and troughs, so plan to sell at the top of a peak. You may face a dilemma if you want the authorities to believe that you are only just getting by, whilst simultaneously convincing buyers of the vast profits. As in all business dealings, honesty is the best policy and allows you to sleep at night. And, of course, you will naturally keep all your assets in tip-top condition to maximise their resale value.

So far, we have considered the situation where you *choose* the time to move on. You may receive an unsolicited offer at any time from someone who wants to buy you out. They may wish to merge your enterprise with their own as a means of growing, they may want to eliminate you as competition or they may simply have acquisition funds they wish to invest in a going concern.

DIAGNOSTIC QUESTION BOX
What price is your business worth if put on the market today?

Although there are many honest potential buyers, there are also a few sharks in these waters. These predators make a killing by buying up businesses at the lowest possible price, stripping all their assets and then selling the site and premises. Their aim is to recover the purchase price as soon as possible – usually from selling the assets – and the rest is their profit.

Even though there are laws to protect the staff of any business sold as a going concern, these predators are adept at finding ways around them. If you have staff, you have a moral duty to ensure their well-being as far as you can. Sharks are great at due diligence when they investigate your books and profit potential. If you receive an unexpected offer, you must do similar due diligence concerning the potential buyer's background and track record. Proceed with care and always take qualified legal advice. Never sign anything that looks like a letter of agreement without running it past your lawyer first. Never sign any document without first reading it and understanding it.

As an entrepreneur you may operate as a sole trader or limited company. This usually means that the buck stops with you. If you have a partnership, joint ownership, shareholders or other stakeholders, each of these will have a vested and financial interest in the negotiations and outcomes of any proposed sale. Be aware that partners can slow down or even prevent your plans from coming to fruition, so keep all parties informed and onside at all times.

What are the components of the company's true sales value? Premises, machinery, office equipment and other tangibles are easily recognised and can be professionally valued, although you should be aware that, apart from premises or land, the second-hand perceived value of other assets may be far lower than you might expect.

Now we enter a somewhat foggy area. If you have a brand name that is recognised within your industry or business specialism, this too will have a value. If the owners were ever to sell the Google, Coca Cola or McDonalds brand names we would clearly be talking of billions of dollars. Fred's Fizzy Drinks or Joe's Burgers might not attract such value. There are exceptions such as Ben & Jerry's ice cream which started as an unknown brand and is now a worldwide success.

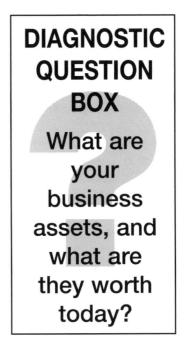

DIAGNOSTIC QUESTION BOX

What are your business assets, and what are they worth today?

Consider a strong brand for your business as this could enhance its ultimate value for your get-out planning strategy. Goodwill is another misty area that is almost impossible to value scientifically. It is made even more difficult because it can vanish overnight as a result of some catastrophic bad news story in the media. It has been claimed that Gerald Ratner destroyed his business when he admitted that most of his jewellery was 'crap' and, as a result, customer goodwill evaporated. The value of goodwill is always negotiable. You will see it as high; your buyer may see it as insignificant. The truth is usually somewhere in the middle. Be realistic and pragmatic about its true worth.

Your sale may include stock, raw materials, part completed orders and unsold stock. Again, an independent professional adviser is essential, and do not let your buyer choose the stocktaker firm, auditor or valuer. If you cannot mutually agree on one, let them use theirs, you use yours and then, together, look for the middle ground.

The independent service professional often has no stock as such. The only tangible asset may be a list of customers or clients which will rapidly become out of date, or in the case of something like a temping agency, ad hoc workers on their books. They can still, however, create a brand. In Britain, Office Angels has grown into a name that has a significant reputation and goodwill value.

If you are a therapist, trainer, consultant, coach, public speaker or other professional practitioner, you will do well to incorporate some provision for tangible products as you create your practice. These can be along the lines of books, audio programmes, aromatherapy oils or whatever products have an appeal to your clients. These will add to your turnover and profits and then, when you sell, you have something that can be counted and valued. Another route could be to train others in your speciality and then allow

DIAGNOSTIC QUESTION BOX

What is your brand and could you sell it?

them to use your name as franchisees. This could, of course, have a brand value and a measurable profit input from selling franchises, licence fees and collecting any royalties included in such arrangements.

An artist or photographer could build a portfolio of limited edition prints that can be sold to collectors or galleries and create a residual income that, again, can be valued.

Timing is all important. You must know when to sell. In the early 1970s a keen music lover started a tape cassette rental business. It thrived and had a good sales potential until CDs were invented and became so cheap that nobody would even think of renting cassettes. If he had continued, recent download technology would have got him in the end. Book and video libraries are similarly facing being overtaken by technological advances.

It would be hard to find buyers for a teleprinter or duplicating machine manufacturer. Cobblers, tinkers, knife-sharpeners and radio repair shops have all been forced out of business by our current 'throwaway culture' where it is often cheaper to replace than to repair. Even independent pharmacies are facing threats from in-store supermarket competition. In the photographic business, developing and printing services are vanishing daily, along with film manufacturing and related accessories, as digital technology replaces traditional chemical-based processes.

The message is clear. You must keep an eye open for developments and social trends that could adversely impact on the value of your business. This will help you to stay up to speed – or to get out before it is too late. Keep an eye on the business pages of your favourite daily paper and, instead of letting those trade papers and magazines pile up on the window sill, actually read them for some trend spotting. Of course, there is a third way. There will always be a niche market for traditional products and skills; witness today's healthy sales for record players, many years after vinyl ceased to be the main recording

DIAGNOSTIC QUESTION BOX

How do you keep informed of the trends in your industry?

medium. Yesterday's technology may still be cutting edge and state-of-the-art in some less developed countries, where it can be traded for goods that are not readily available at home and so yield another measurable value.

There is no single and ultimate get-out plan that can be universally applied. Some retired entrepreneurs have stayed on for an agreed period as consultants or mentors to new business owners. In cases of passing a family business down to the next generation, a gradual transition is sometimes possible, where the father (or mother) figure takes an ever-reducing part in the running of the business as the responsibilities of their offspring proportionately increase. This is perhaps an ideal situation, but one thing is abundantly clear: you must have a succession plan in place and it must be regularly reviewed and updated. You might even hold the thought that the main reason for starting a business is to sell it and enjoy the fruits of your labours!

Diagnostic Action Box

1. Plan your succession arrangements when you plan your business

2. Consider how you can add value for the day you choose to sell

3. Branding can be sold as well as goodwill, so work on yours

4. Treat any unsolicited offers to buy your business with extreme caution

5. Involve all stakeholders in your succession planning

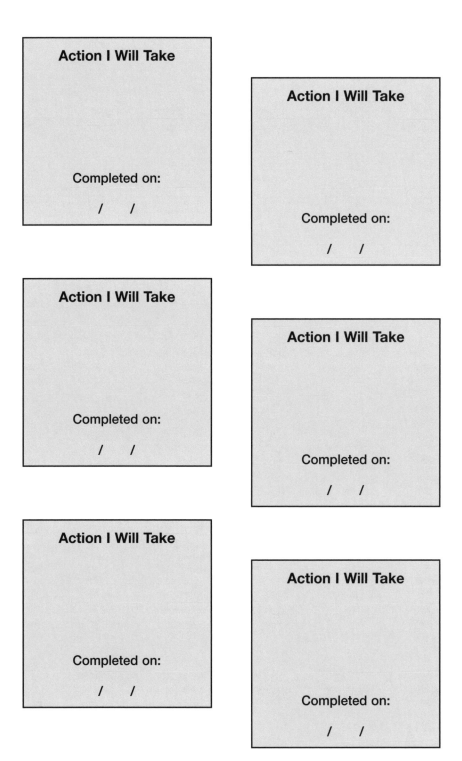

Action I Will Take

Completed on:

/   /

Action I Will Take

Completed on:

/   /

Action I Will Take

Completed on:

/   /

Action I Will Take

Completed on:

/   /

Action I Will Take

Completed on:

/   /

Action I Will Take

Completed on:

/   /

Bibliography

Abraham, J., *Money-Making Secrets of Marketing Genius Jay Abraham and Other Marketing Wizards*, Abraham, 1993

Adams, R., *A Good Hard Kick in the Ass,* Century, 2002

Ashton, R., *The Entrepreneur's Book of Checklists*, 2004

Beckwith, H., *Selling The Invisible,* Thomson Texere, 2002

Blanchard, K., *The One Minute Manager*, HarperCollins, 2000

Clayton, P., *Forming a Limited Company*, Kogan Press 2006

Covey, S., *Seven Habits of Highly Effective People*, Simon & Schuster, 1989.

Francis, J., *Price Yourself Right*, Universe, 2006

Gerber, M, E., *The E-Myth Manager*, Harper Business, 1999

Hayden, C.J., *Get Clients Now*, Amacom, 1999

Kennedy, G., *Everything is Negotiable*, Century Business 1989

Martin, C., *The Life Coaching Handbook*, Crown House Publishing, 2001

Mehrabian, A., *Silent Messages*, Wadsworth, 1971.

Messmer, M., *Motivating Employees for Dummies*, Hungry Minds Inc, 2001

Rowson, P., *Marketing*, Rowmark, 1999

Sempler, R., *Maverick*, Century, 1993

Sercombe, A., *Me & Co*, Word Publishing, 2001

Smith, R., *Up Your Aspirations*, Pau, 1996

Souton, M., West, C., *The Beermat Entreprenuer*, Prentice Hall 2006

The Essential Business Guide Ltd, *The Essential Business Guide*, 2005

Woods, C., *From Acorns...*, Prentice Hall, 2003

Author Resource Guide

If you would like to contact Curly Martin you can do so through the publisher or directly using the contact details below. If you visit the website you will find an abundant resource and opportunity to join a forum for business discussions. There will be regular business coaching reminders delivered to your computer keeping you on tract as you take your business to the next level of business growth. Visit now and take advantage of all there is on offer.

E-mail: contact@businesscoachingdirect.co.uk
Website: www.businesscoachingdirect.co.uk
Telephone: 44 (0)1202 255898

> Curly Martin – Founder of:
> Achievement Specialists Ltd.
> Achievement House,
> 100 Southwick Road
> Bournemouth
> BH6 5PU

Curly welcomes discussions and is happy to answer any questions you may have about the book or website.

Index